WHY
I BELIEVE
IN
MEDJUGORJE

Medjugorje Explained

Father Livio Fanzaga

About the Author

Fr. Livio Fanzaga was born in Fergamo, Italy. In 1987 he became director of programming at Radio Maria. At that time the station was just a small local Catholic broadcaster. Today the world family of Radio Maria is the largest international Catholic radio network. Fr. Livio continues to be its director. He has also authored over 20 books on different religious topics including many on Medjugorje.

Translated from the Italian by Lou and Michelle Iacobelli.

Throughout the book, the words "man," "men," "mankind," "he," ""his," "himself," "brothers," "sons," etc. are denoted as being all-inclusive, respecting both genders, as the context requires.

Published 2012 in English by:
Ave Maria Centre of Peace,
P.O. Box 489, Station U, Toronto, ON, M8Z 5Y8 Canada
P.O. Box 375, Niagara Falls, NY 14304-0375 USA

ISBN #978-1-927108-03-1

Printed and bound in Canada by Ave Maria Centre of Peace

Table of Contents

CHAPTER 1

I have chosen this parish in a special way

MEDJUGORJE IS THE PARISH OF MARY

I remember as if it were now. The first time I heard people talk about Medjugorje (already in the first months of the apparitions) which had started June 24th 1981. I was having dinner with a priest-friend of mine, who had just come back from a nearby school where he had been teaching religion, and he said that in class they had told him about an unusual event which had happened in an unknown village of Yugoslavia. There, some youngsters were saying that they were seeing the Madonna (Virgin Mary) daily.

It was in that circumstance that I heard (for the first time) the name of Medjugorje and quickly the unusual event attracted my attention. Immediately I felt a profound and unexplainable joy. I have always been more or less devoted to the Madonna, even if the circumstances of life had never brought me to visit famous shrines like Lourdes or Fatima. When I heard mention of the name of this location of Herzegovina, I felt an insurmountable desire to go and visit it.

After many years, thinking back to that moment, I understand how the conviction of the pilgrims who go to Medjugorje is true; they are personally called there by Mary. One doesn't go to Medjugorje as one might go to any other shrine; even the most important or the most holy. It would be more accurate to state that one is compelled to go to Medjugorje mysteriously by an invisible hand, for grace through unexplainable circumstances guides one's steps toward this privileged place.

For me, the time of the first pilgrimage were quite long. At that period, Yugoslavia was a communist country, where religion was not easily tolerated. I experienced first-hand the ever-present secret and obvious police-presence which controlled the area. As time passed, the facts of Medjugorje were beginning to interest and intrigue many people, including those far from the faith.

The bishop of Mostar, after a first favourable phase, was spreading his contrary ideas about the apparitions throughout the world. The discussions were very intense but the people were beginning to spontaneously organize the first pilgrimages. Quite quickly the unstoppable river of pilgrims began to flow from every part of the world, even from outside Yugoslavia.

It was in the middle of March of 1985 that I organized my first trip by car along with two young people from my parish of St. Giuseppe Calasanzio in Milan, one of which had been to Medjugorje a few months before. I was hoping to enjoy the first signs of spring along the Dalmatian Coast but we passed a whole week under an unrelenting, never-ending rainfall. The roads were criss-crossed by waterfalls which carried rocks and soil down from the mountains. The voyage seemed unending. I asked myself: why did the Madonna choose a country so far away? Then, I still didn't realize that even the Pope came from a far-away, Slavic-speaking country.

At nightfall we finally arrived at the entrance of the leveled area of Medjugorje. Then, it was a collection of small villages situated at the foot of the hills. There were no new houses nor any shops or places for resting, which are now spread out here and there with a disorder typically Mediterranean. Everywhere we would see fields cultivated with tobacco or grapes. Surrounding this were the silence and the austere poverty of many farmhouses. But here, suddenly appearing on the horizon, was the parochial church between two bell towers. It was rising like a small cathedral in an immense bowl populated by greenery. We had finally arrived in Medjugorje, Mary's parish.

TO BELIEVE IN THE APPARITIONS IS A GRACE

One could discuss forever about so-called private apparitions, in a particular way how they attract the consciences of the faithful and about what value the Church should give them. The same denomination of "private apparition" does not satisfy at all because they are often a public event with a clear ecclesiastic profile. Some, rightly so, propose to call them "extra-biblical revelations" to distinguish them from biblical revelations.

The Church however gives them a certain importance, affirming that real and correct fountains of spirituality coming from this type of revelation have sprinkled the Christian community with grace. One thinks, for example of the devotion to the Sacred Heart fed by Saint Margaret Mary Alacoque and from St. Faustina Kowalska.

Belief in these events of supernatural character is in my opinion and according to my own experience, a gift of grace. When I arrived in Medjugorje, I quickly found confirmation of what my heart had foreseen from the beginning. Getting out of the car we entered the church while they were reciting the rosary before the evening Mass. A heavenly choir in the Croatian language resounded in a temple brimming with people. In those days the people were for the most part from the area. In spite of the rain, the wind and the darkness, all the benches were occupied by the farmers of the area, men and women, youths and children. It was a weekday, but this spectacle was something we were not used to seeing even on Sundays.

Medjugorje in the early days.

I entered the church and I dressed for the Holy Mass. We were four concelebrants; a number certainly not comparable to the actual number of several dozen priests from every part of the world that daily come to the parish church. From high up on the altar I saw the forest of faces burned by the wind and the sun but full of dignity and absorbed in prayer. I did not understand one word, but I felt myself in profound harmony. In that moment, I understood that Medjugorje was, before everything, a community in prayer.

Before the beginning of the Holy Mass a door on my left side suddenly opened, the door facing the sacristy, and from there came the small clean and smiling face of Marija.[1] Behind her, I saw the serious face of Ivan and the jaunty face of Jakov. The apparition had just finished. From that time, I have been able to be present in many apparitions of the Madonna and God only knows how many graces and spiritual emotions they have given me. In that circumstance however I had a unique and unrepeatable experience.

What was this all about? In the light of the soul I had the grace, the certainty that the Madonna was really appearing and hence Christianity is the only true religion. I don't want anyone to misunderstand me. God forbid that a priest would not be certain of the truth of his religion! But it is one thing to believe with your intelligence and another to believe it with your heart. One cannot describe the experience that one has when a truth pierces you completely and takes possession of your life.

In those days, I was reading many books about all the important religions. I would make comparisons; I sought affinities among the various beliefs and at the same time I would increase the reasons for the superiority of our beliefs compared to that of the others. In that moment however, it was like the entire Christian belief had become flesh in the body of Marija, a person alive and true, who three minutes before had appeared to three youngsters a few meters from me.

I celebrated the Mass in a different way than usual. Never like that time had I felt the presence of Jesus on the altar. *"Unceasingly adore the Most Blessed Sacrament of the Altar. I am always present when the faithful are adoring"* the Holy Mother had said exactly a year before. (March 15/84) The truths of the faith were dressing themselves in new clothes before my mind of flesh and bones and everything seemed to me brighter and simpler. How much study, how many discussions, how many books to strengthen the faith! An invisible touch of grace had obtained infinitely much more.

Was it necessary to go to Medjugorje to live this spiritual experience? It is difficult to answer this. God always acts with supreme liberty. How many pilgrims, however, could give testimony to having been touched by grace having once arrived in that blessed place? The same trip is an internal exodus that is undertaken in the midst of many spiritual and material difficulties. The grace that one receives upon getting there is a special gift for having responded to the call.

It is not necessary to marvel at what the pilgrims tell when they return. It is not unusual that even doubtful and skeptical priests return full of fervor and changed, even to the great amazement of their parishioners. It is not excitement. Medjugorje is just a parish to which the Madonna, like she herself has said on different occasions, has granted particular graces.

THE CHURCH LEAVES US FREE TO BELIEVE

Bishop Zanic

The next day I decided to go to Mostar to visit the cathedral and if possible to visit the then bishop, Monsignor Zanic. It was universally noted that he opposed the apparitions, a change from when, in the first two months, he had publically defended the visionaries. The visionaries were two boys and four girls and he had affirmed that they were not lying. His sudden change of opinion has always remained a mystery. Let us not forget that the context was that of a communist country, well intended to suffocating phenomena of this nature at birth. Later on I saw in action, with my own eyes, the secret police of Sarajevo with their very effective methods of persuasion.

The cathedral of Mostar was a modern church which showed off to the sky the proud subjugation of reinforced concrete. Beside it the framed squat profile of the Episcopal palace, also of recent construction, acted as its guardian. I was fortunate. The bishop was at the entrance talking to a Franciscan friar. Mons. Zanic was a sociable and cordial type. I opened the discussion saying that I had come to Medjugorje attracted by the fame of the apparitions. He said that he was

Mostar Cathedral circa 1989.

returning from Lourdes and showed me a beautiful statue of the Madonna that he had put on prominent display in the cathedral. He was interested in showing himself to be Marian but concluded by saying that the apparitions of Medjugorje were an invention of the friars.

I remained perplexed as to what to reply. He tried to convince me by introducing me to the friar who was beside him. He was the Father Provincial of the Franciscans. "Look", he said to me, "even he doesn't believe in it." The father provincial displayed a courteous smile. It was

11

1985. Six years later the cathedral of Mostar as well as the convent of the Franciscans were pitilessly razed to the ground by Serbian bombs.

Bishop Zanic was very correct. He told me that in the absence of official pronouncements from the Church, I was free to believe or not to believe in the apparitions. Then he also stated that eventually we would have to submit to any disciplinary actions. I asked myself what was brewing. A short time later a notice appeared from the Congregation for the Faith published in "L'Osservatore Romano" and signed by Mons. Bovono, then secretary of the same Congregation. Official pilgrimages were forbidden but those organized privately were allowed.

Mostar in pre-war days.

From then nothing has changed in the Church's attitude. The Queen of Peace had chosen a parish for herself with a pastor appointed by a bishop and a community of religious authorized by him to exercise the pastoral ministry. The Church through her representatives in the various levels, some of them against, others instead friendly, has limited itself to observe the phenomenon, whose aspects from the pastoral point of view could not be ignored.

Lately I have reflected much on the divine strategy of Mary put into action in Medjugorje. In a different way than La Salette, Lourdes, Fatima and many other apparitions, here in Medjugorje the Madonna took a parish for herself as if she herself were the pastor. Certainly, even here she has chosen some young people as she is frequently wont to do. But here they are inserted within the parish and the messages themselves, via the visionaries, are given to the parish. The Madonna, also much later, when the followers of the Queen of Peace were dispersed all the world, has specified that the messages are first given to the parish and then to all others.

A particular, apparently insignificant, but very instructive event has struck me. Consider that Marija, the visionary who receives the regular messages of the 25th of the month from the Madonna, has now established her residence in Italy.

What does all this mean? It is truly a new way of Mary manifesting herself. Not only considering the length of time but also regarding the methods of the messages. Never in the past has the Madonna taken a personal interest in a parish, inserting herself intimately in the ecclesiastic institution. The faithful who go to Medjugorje know that they are going to a very familiar place. That is, to a parish church with a pastor regularly named by the bishop and where the priests in the confessionals absolve with the authority of the Church.

In Medjugorje, there have been a variety of pastors, but all have been favourable to the apparitions. The same can be said of the various friars that have been part of the parish. Among the parishioners, I have never met one who has been against the apparitions, except an activist of the party in the first years, before the fall of communism. Here it is not just about a supernatural phenomenon that interests a few youngsters, but of something much greater and more involving. Because the Madonna has decided to take a personal interest in a parish, this represents a fundamental question for understanding her plan.

For some time I am arrested by these thoughts, trying to enter into the heart of an event that has no comparison in the course of history. Even that first Thursday of my stay in Medjugorje, the message rang out like this: *"Dear children I love you and in a special way I have chosen this parish, one more dear to me than the others, in which I have gladly remained when the Almighty sent me."* (March 21/85) I asked myself what could this preference be attributed to. Later on I understood that through Medjugorje, Mary intended to reawaken the faith in all Christian parishes and to increasingly make the Church, of which she is mother, her great parish.

CHAPTER 2

My angels

ARE THE VISIONARIES CREDIBLE?

I had the opportunity to get to know the visionaries of Medjugorje when they were still youngsters. Now they are fully grown men and women, each one with their own family. There is no doubt that the most eloquent sign of the presence of the Madonna in Medjugorje are just these six young people from whom she asked much, entrusting to them a mission that, because of its nature, requires great generosity.

Any person with common sense would have to ask himself how six youngsters, each so different and with his own life concerns, in spite of a deep cordiality which unites them, could testify for such a long time about the daily apparitions of the Mother of God, without any contradictions, without confusion and without changing their minds.

At the time scientific experiments were carried out by clearly qualified medical teams who came to the conclusion that there weren't any hallucinations involved and confirmed the inexplicability under a purely scientific profile, of the phenomena tied to the apparitions. It seems that on one occasion the Madonna had said that such experiments were not necessary. Effectively, the simple observation of the psychological normality of the young people is enough; their own equilibrium and progressive human and spiritual maturity will in time conclude that this is all about very reliable testimony.

The six Medjugorje visionaries during the early days.

An English proverb states that in order to know a person well one must eat a bushel of salt with them. I ask myself how many bags of salt the inhabitants of Medjugorje have eaten with these youngsters. I have never heard a person from the place doubt them. And also how many mothers and how many fathers would have wished that their son or daughter would be chosen as testimonies of the Virgin Mary! In what country in the world are there not rivalries, small jealousies and contrasting interests? Nevertheless, no one in Medjugorje has even placed in doubt that the Madonna has chosen these six and not others. Among the boys and girls of Medjugorje, there have never been other visionary candidates. Dangers of this kind have perhaps come from elsewhere.

It is necessary above all to give some attention to the families of Bijakovici, the small hamlet within Medjugorje from which the visionaries come, for having accepted with discipline the choice of the Gospa, the name there given to the Madonna, without complaining and without ever questioning this choice. Satan, to enact his tortuous intrigues, has always had to rely on strangers, finding the people of the area solid.

The time that passes is a great gentleman. If something isn't right, sooner or later it comes to light. Truth has long legs and this is seen when we calmly examine a period of time that is now over 30+ years of daily apparitions. It concerns among other things, the more difficult periods in life, that of adolescence and youth, from fifteen to thirty years. These are tempestuous years, subject to unexpected evolutions. Whoever has children knows very well what this means.

And still the young people of Medjugorje have traveled this long road without any dimming or eclipses of faith and without a moral fall. Whoever knows the facts well knows what weights they have had to carry from the beginning, when the communist regime was persecuting them in various ways, stalking them, preventing them from climbing the mountain of the apparitions and even trying to suggest that they were mental invalids. In essence, they were only youngsters. They thought that it would be enough if they intimidated them. Once I witnessed a blitz from the secret police that carried Vicka and Marija away for interrogation. The climate of the first years was thick with threats. The daily meeting with the heavenly Mother has always been the true strength that has sustained them.

To this is added the hostility of the local bishop, whose attitude, however one evaluates it, has represented and to this day represents a heavy cross to bear. One of the visionaries once said to me, almost in tears, "The bishop insists that I am a liar." Another thorn in the side of Medjugorje is constituted by the hostile attitude of several ecclesiastic attitudes and God only knows why in His wise kingdom has wanted that the parish, and in the first place, the visionaries, have to carry this cross.

There have been years of navigation through the waves of an ocean more or less in agitation. But all of this is nothing before the daily task of receiving the pilgrims.

From the first days of the apparitions there arrived thousands from all of Croatia and elsewhere. Then began the full unstoppable arrival of visitors from every part of the world. From the early morning hours the homes of the visionaries were assaulted by people who prayed, questioned, and most of all hoped that the Madonna would bend to their necessities.

From 1985 I have spent all my holidays, a month of the year, in Medjugorje to help some of the visionaries welcome the pilgrims. From morning till night these youngsters, particularly Vicka and Marija, welcomed groups, repeated the messages, listened to petitions, prayed with the people. The languages were mixed, hands were interlaced, the notes of requests for the Madonna accumulated, the sick begged, the most over-excited naturally in first place, the Italians, almost overtook the houses of the vision-

Vicka greeting the pilgrims.

aries. I ask myself how the families have been able to survive in the midst of this unceasing siege.

Then, near evening, when the people would swarm toward the church, here was finally the moment of prayers and the apparitions; a rest without which the seers couldn't go on. Then there is the dinner to prepare, the friends, the relatives and the acquaintances invited to the table to serve, the dishes to wash, and finally, almost always, attending the prayer group until late at night.

Which young person would have been able to survive this type of life? Who would have attempted it? Who would not have lost his psychological equilibrium? However, after many years you find in front of you people who are serene, calm and balanced, certain of what they say, humanly understanding, aware of their mission. They have their limits and their defects, fortunately, but they are simple, clear and humble. They are the six youngsters, the first and the most precious sign of the presence of the Madonna in Medjugorje.

THE COMPONENTS OF THE GROUP

The first day, June 24, 1981, four of them saw the Madonna: Ivanka, Mirjana, Vicka and Ivan. Milka, Marija's sister also saw her. But the next day to the original four were added Marija, and Jakov, while Milka was at work and in this way, the group was complete. The Madonna considers June 24th, feast of St. John the Baptist, a day of preparation, while the anniversary of the apparitions is considered to be the 25th of June. From 1987 the Madonna has begun to give the messages every 25th of the month, almost to underline the particular significance of this day which remembers the great festivities of the Annunciation (March 25) and of Christmas (December 25).

The Mother of God first appeared on the hill of Podbrdo at whose feet lay the houses of Bijakovici, while the visionaries were on the road which today many pilgrims travel to arrive at the 'Field of Life' of the children of Sr. Elvira. The Madonna was motioning them to approach closer, but the young visionaries were paralyzed by fear and joy at the same time. In the following days the apparitions changed towards the actual place of the mountain and despite the boulders and the tightly growing bushes of very prickly thorns, the encounters with the

Site of the first apparition on Mount Podbrdo.

Madonna were happening at a closer distance, while a growing number of persons, counted in the thousands, would crowd around them.

From that 25th of June the group of visionaries has remained unchanged, even if only three of them have the apparitions every day. In fact, Mirjana from Christmas 1982 stopped having daily apparitions and meets the Madonna every 18th of March on her birthday.[2] Ivanka, however, meets the Madonna every 25th of June since her daily visions stopped May 7, 1985. Jakov's daily visions stopped on Sept. 12, 1998 and will have an apparition of the Madonna every Christmas.

It is therefore assumed that the Gospa moves very liberally with the visionaries, in the sense that these directions are not binding for her. From Vicka, for example, she has asked six times for an interruption of the apparitions (four of forty days and two of forty-five days) as a sacrifice to offer.

I have noticed that the six people chosen by the Madonna, even having among themselves more or less rare contacts and being now spread throughout the world, feel themselves to be a compact group. They have much respect for each other and never have I caught them in contradictions. They are perfectly aware of living the same experience, even if each of them has his own personal way of testifying it.

Sometimes, people from the area have approached the six visionaries with charisms of another nature, like interior messages. This concerns very different phenomena among them that must be considered apart. The Church, on the other hand, makes pronouncements about the apparitions while it does not examine the existence of interior locutions

Neither has been a shortage of other visionaries who have come from other places pretending to unite themselves to the seers. One of the dangers that pilgrims face is to encounter some prestigious personality who presents messages as if they were coming from them the Madonna of Medjugorje. But these messages come from other sources or other supposed visionaries, which have nothing to do with these six young people chosen for the apparitions. A failure to clarify this point by those in Medjugorje who have the duty to be vigilant about these factors could hurt the cause.

The Madonna has constantly protected her six 'angels' as she called them in the early years, and has always impeded the clever attempts studied by Satan, the untiring falsifier, to alter the group, adding or substituting its members. From the beginning the Church has been clear, such that the bishop at first and the Croatian Commission of the

Episcopal Conference later have limited the extent of their examinations to the group formed by the Mother of God on June 25, 1981.

On this point it is necessary to have very clear ideas. For her great plan, Mary has chosen an actual parish and six youngsters who live there. These are her decisions, which must be respected as do the people in the area. Whatever attempt to change the cards on the table can be ascribed to the eternal liar who works, as always, through human ambitions.

THE MISSION OF THE SIX VISIONARIES

By knowing the visionaries of Medjugorje I have been able to discover their great joy, enduring all this time, for having been chosen by Mary. Who wouldn't be? They are aware of having received a great grace, but at the same time of carrying a great responsibility on their shoulders. As in La Salette, Lourdes and Fatima, the Mother of God has demonstrated that she selects the poor, the small and the simple for great work. The social and familial context of these apparitions is very similar. They are farming families in very poor areas where, however, a solid and sincere faith is still alive.

Now the social situation in Medjugorje has improved. The influx of pilgrims and their reception in homes has brought a certain wellbeing. Construction activities have increased land value. The majority of the families, including those of the visionaries, have rebuilt or newly-built their own house. House and work are part of the daily bread that every Christian asks from the Heavenly Father.

The parish has notably increased its facilities for welcoming thanks to the offerings of the pilgrims. Altogether however, the portrait is not one of wealth but of a dignified life where the only work available is tied to the pilgrimages.

At the beginning the situation was much different. The context was of difficult farm work and a grey and difficult poverty. The Madonna loves to choose her most precious collaborators from these environments. She herself was a small child of an unknown village when God showed His predilection on her. It remains a mystery hidden in the heart of Mary why her gaze has landed on this parish and on these six particular individuals.

We are brought to think that particular gifts have to be merited and whoever receives them is favoured. When we receive graces or special charisms we ask ourselves, "But what have I done to deserve this?" From that moment we look at ourselves with other eyes, searching to find merits that we didn't know we had. In reality God chooses His instruments with sovereign liberty and, in many occasions, rescuing them from the dust bin.

Graces of this kind are not merited and the real problem is that of responding with faithfulness and humility, knowing that others, in our place, could do a much better job. On the other hand, the Madonna herself has on many occasions pointed out that each of us has an important place in God's plan for the salvation of the world.

To the question posed by the visionaries of why the Madonna has chosen them, the Madonna answered letting them understand that they were neither better nor worse than the others. As to the choosing of the parishioners, the Virgin has wanted to underline that she had chosen them as they were, that is, with their negative and positive qualities. In these answers, the condition of normality seems to appear. The youth chosen by Mary were not the most ardent in the practice of their religion. Many others were going to church more than they were.

On the other hand, it can be noted that Bernadette was excluded from First Communion for her lack of knowledge of the catechism. We also know in what rushed ways the little shepherds of Fatima would pray the rosary before the apparitions. At La Salette, the situation is even more uncertain because the two visionaries did not even recite their morning or evening prayers.

Whoever receives an assignment also receives the graces necessary for their accomplishment. The Madonna sees hearts and knows how to extract the best from each of us. To the young people of Medjugorje she has entrusted a mission whose fullness and importance has not yet fully manifested itself. It has never happened in public apparitions that the Virgin has asked for a commitment so intense and lengthy, such that it absorbs the entire life of a person.

It is an assignment which asks for fidelity, courage, a spirit of sacrifice, constancy and perseverance. We ask ourselves whether this extraordinary mission entrusted to these very young people would be fully accomplished. In this regard, the answer is only one: the youngsters, now adults, have responded in the best way possible.

God does not expect them to reach the peak of holiness by forced stages. The two shepherds of La Salette will never be elevated to the honours of the altar. Their life has been more than arduous. They have, however, accomplished their mission perfectly, in the greatest fidelity, remaining loyal in their testimony of the message received even till the end.

Even the saints have their own defects. Imagine these youngsters still at the beginning of their spiritual journeys. In this type of mission, two fundamental virtues count: humility and fidelity. The first is the evangelical awareness of being useless and defective servants. The second is the courage of testifying the gift received without ever denying it. The visionaries of Medjugorje, as I know them, even with their limits and defects, are humble and faithful. Only God knows how saintly they are. This, on the other hand, is true for everyone. Sainthood is a long walk which we are called to walk until the last instant of our lives.

I have been very impressed by what the biographers have written about St. Joan of Arc. After she had avoided the flames by signing a document of renunciation which had been requested by the ecclesiastic college which was judging her, the interior 'voices' which were guiding her advised her that if she did not testify to the mission which God had entrusted to her, she would have been eternally lost.

The Madonna can be well content by the adolescents which she has chosen so long ago. Now they are adults, mothers and fathers of families, but every day they welcome her invitation and witness for her before a world so often distracted, incredulous and mocking.

Some would ask why all of the six visionaries of the apparitions have married, while none have consecrated themselves completely to God according to the ordinary ways of the Church.

In this regard, it should be noted that from the first apparitions, to the visionaries who were asking for advice for their state in life, the Madonna replied that it would have been good to consecrate themselves completely to the Lord, but in any case they were completely free to choose. Effectively, Ivan entered the seminary but was not able to continue because of the many gaps in his studies. Marija in her turn had long wished to enter the convent, without ever having the interior certainty for the way that God would show her.

In the end, six have chosen matrimony which, let's not forget, is the ordinary way to sanctity, and which in particular needs to be testified. It is a choice certainly preset from heaven. Also, thinking about it, allows the visionaries to be available for Mary's plans which they wouldn't be able to do if they were in the rigid structures of the consecrated life. For the Madonna it is important that the young people she has chosen be witnesses of her presence before the Church and the world and that their actual situation is the most suitable for that purpose.

CHAPTER 3

This is a time of great graces

GOD BREAKS THE SILENCE

I have asked myself at various times why the apparitions have such a deep impact on people and not only on those who attend church. In fact, they often attract the attention of those far away from the Church. At times even the non-Catholics, as has happened in Medjugorje, which has seen the presence not only of many lost lambs of the Catholic flock, but also that of the Protestants, Orthodox and Muslims. The apparition in itself contains an important message which people of any category grasp, even subconsciously.

The Church, at least at the beginning, was skeptical but the people rushed to come. The pastor of those first days, Father Jozo Zovko, used to walk up and down the empty church while thousands of people climbed among the thorns and rocks of Podbrdo, the hill where the Madonna first appeared to the youngsters. The same had happened to the pastors of Lourdes and Fatima. The same people who are lukewarm to the call of the parish bells don't care about any difficulties, except to be present in the places where Mary is appearing. Still, they see noth-

Fr. Jozo with five of the visionaries.

ing in particular, but through the person of the visionary, there is the sensation of almost seeing and touching the supernatural.

Is it something negative under the outline of the faith? Absolutely not. Indeed we must not forget that the apparition of the risen Christ was able to revive the dead faith of the apostles and the first disciples. Thinking about it carefully, apparitions are part of Christianity. They accompany the walk of faith of the Church from its beginning.

Certainly the apparitions of the Risen Christ have a unique value and constitute for Christians of every age an object of divine faith. To be Christians it is necessary to believe in the testimony of the apostles who affirm that Jesus is risen and has appeared to them.

Indeed, even from the beginning Jesus has sustained the path of His Church with frequent apparitions, which we would call private revelations today, with which He would comfort and guide the apostles, the missionaries of the gospel, the virgins and the martyrs. All of this does not eliminate the walk of faith, but illuminates it, encourages it and makes it more immediate. In the last centuries a certain rationalistic mentality which has hardened quite a few men of the Church. It has created a climate of suspicion of supernatural phenomena, often considered with annoyance and snobbery even when the Church has evaluated them positively.

In the past and for many centuries it was not so. Let us think only of the thousands of Marian shrines in every part of the world where the faithful with great sacrifices have wanted to render perennial testimony to the appearance of Mary. Let us contemplate the life of many saints who had the great joy of meeting with the Lord and with Mary, with whom they often had a daily intimate familiarity. There is no doubt that an apparition is not something rare and exceptional in the life of the Church. On the contrary, it is part of an economy that God has frequently used in His relationship with mankind, stopping and confirming the teaching way of the faith.

Faith is a difficult walk. If it is not fed by prayer and from the intimate union with God, it risks becoming a smoking wick, always on the point of extinguishing itself. The flesh does not understand the things of above and it seduces man again into the closed circle of finite things. The world is unbelieving and sows in the hearts of the faithful doubts and apprehension. Gods seems to be silent, and His silence leaves in astonishment those who live on this minuscule planet wrapped in immense and indecipherable space.

Who of the faithful doesn't ask in certain moments of his life: God, where are you? Why are you silent? Why are you hiding? Why don't you show yourself? Our times have seen the most amazing eclipses of God since the world was created. Mankind, according to what the Madonna states in Medjugorje, is constructing a *"new world without God"* only with his own efforts and because of this, he is unhappy and without joy in his heart.

The darkness, doubt, insecurity and distress for the future penetrate consciences. The faith of many vacillates under the pressure of a pagan, atheistic, materialistic and egoistic mentality.

It is in this spiritual tempest that the apparitions of the Madonna in Medjugorje are located. They constitute the merciful response of God in a moment of great spiritual bewilderment of humanity. Their duration is proportional to the vastness of the work that the Madonna has wished to take on for the good of the Church and the world. They are located in the wake of the list of the numerous interventions of Mary in the course of the centuries. At the same time they are important and are manifested with a newness which we cannot fully evaluate, located as they are in an epic passage that has no equal in the travels of humanity.

In our times we are given to be witnesses of one of the greatest manifestations of God through Mary that have ever occurred in the story of Christianity.

THE APPARITIONS OF MARY ARE A GREAT GRACE

An abstract discussion of the apparitions risks treating them with indifference. Touching them with our hands instead, shocks and moves us. Whoever has been present at an apparition, remaining always in the regime of faith, remains profoundly struck. This is a gift of God both for the visionary as for all the rest, present and absent. It is a grave error underestimating them or considering them simply as an individual experience.

The Madonna underlines many times that she has been sent by God for love and her coming among us is a great grace. She laments that we are not aware of the inestimable value of this gift and the messages which she gives us. She reprimands us saying that one day we will lament this long time in which she has been able to instruct us and lead us on the road of salvation.

It is easy, after the initial enthusiasm, to enter into a sort of habit. I have heard many times, and not only in hostile places, a certain unbelief motivated by the excessive duration of these same apparitions. They say that they are lasting too many years and that the Madonna talks too much! Many who hurried there in the beginning have successively become tired, letting themselves be recaptured by the mediocre life of before. Others have swarmed here and there looking for new emotions. The proposal of a voyage of sanctity to follow with perseverance has quickly frightened them.

I have noticed, however, that the visionaries have preserved the fervor of the first days and for them the apparition is a grace which is renewed day to day like sparkling water in which one dips without ever being tired. I ask myself how many are the daily apparitions to which they have assisted? Many thousands, and yet, for them it is like the first time. Meeting the Mother of God is always a grace-filled event. In that moment the skies are opened and who has the gift of seeing Mary enters into a dimension which enraptures.

The supernatural does not tire and cannot become a fact of habit. Every time the Madonna comes, it is like the hereafter bursting into the darkened boundary in which we live and she would wrap our poor life into a divine dimension. No visionary, even after such a long time, would give up even one daily apparition light-heartedly. The Madonna has asked denials of this kind of the visionaries of Medjugorje and they have accepted them for love of her. But it was certainly one of the greatest sacrifices of which the Madonna could ask.

There is nothing to be surprised at. The apparition is an anticipation of the divine life. It is the presence of Paradise on earth. It has a dignity, a simplicity, a beauty that the passing time is not able to disguise or to render commonplace. I have seen the youngsters in ecstasy in the first years of the apparitions and I observed them recently, in a span of over thirty years; the same very high concentration, the same supernatural climate. Their faces are absorbed and serene, their eyes pearls of light; the attitude is that of confident and filial prayer.

Not even once, not even in less favourable situations, have I been able to notice any irreverence or slight inconvenience. An encounter with the Mother of God, when it is authentic, has its own unmistakable imprint. The sky wraps a strip of earth in a divine light and for a few moments our preoccupied and ordinary life enters a new and unknown dimension.

IN THE PRESENCE OF THE MOTHER OF GOD

To be present at an apparition is certainly one of the desires that many cultivate in their hearts when they come to Medjugorje. It has been like this everywhere. Wherever the Madonna appears people gather to pray and to plead for graces. But what is necessary is an act of faith. The visionary with his manner is a sign of the presence of Mary. Finally, whoever is present does not see but believes.

When I arrived for the first time in Medjugorje the youngsters would meet the Madonna in the sacristy of the church; later on, in the choir loft, up high, at the entrance of the same church. Even the priest's house has been, for a while, the place of the apparitions. In the first months instead they would happen ordinarily in the open, on the hill or in other places not identifiable by the police. Often the meeting with the Gospa would happen in houses. Many times a certain number of people would be present. These would later become a real crowd in the night meetings on the hill of the first apparitions, which is called Podbrdo by the people who live there, or at the Blue Cross, at the foot of this same hill. The apparitions of Medjugorje are distinguished by the fact that the Madonna appeared where the visionaries could be found at the moment. They are not tied to a location but to the people. It often happens that the visionaries are found in different parts of the world. Well, the Madonna appears to each of them at the same time. Nevertheless, the hill of the first apparitions is held to be a holy place and represents the most important goal of pilgrimages. There, in fact the Madonna has promised to leave a sign, beautiful, visible and indestructible, which will testify to the world that she has come.

The second time that I went to Medjugorje was in July 1985. It was on that occasion that the desire came to me to be present at an apparition. How to do it? In the previous months the bishop had forbidden the apparitions in the sacristy and now they occurred in a small room of the priest's house, where about twenty people could fit, personally controlled by Father Slavko. I despaired of being one of the chosen in spite of my qualifications as priest. Like in any other part of the world, even there the human factor had a part. In a word, only the usual lucky ones could enter.

I then decided to play my best cards without thought that in cases of this kind it is best to trust in Divine Providence. I went directly to the house of the visionary Marija with whom on the occasion of my first trip I had a good friendship and I asked her to let me enter the room of the apparitions. She tried very hard and was able to let me into the canonical house where there was a tight crowd. But in the hallway, a few metres from the goal, I had to stop in front of an impassable human wall.

It was a very emotional experience just the same. On our knees, tightly squeezed one beside the other, we knew that the Madonna was there while she looked at us and listened to us. If it is true that the visionaries can see the Madonna with eyes of the body, it is also true that all of us can see her with the eyes of the soul. In that instant, with a silence and a superhuman concentration, one can intimately feel the reality of a presence which fills the soul with peace and joy. In the moment of the apparitions, the Mother of God wraps all present with her prayer and gathers them in her heart. Her blessing falls like a balm on the wounds of life.

I was very edified by this experience, which must be considered a grace, even if not all the pilgrims who go to Medjugorje can hope to have it. The whole village is a blessed land and a place of particular graces for those who open their hearts. Later on I had the opportunity to be present at many apparitions both in Medjugorje and in Italy and every time I have thanked the Madonna. I cannot however, forget to tell about the first time that I was present at one of them, having at my disposal the necessary time not only for praying but also for observing the phenomenon in every detail.

It was a hot humid Sunday in July in 1986. I had spent my first

week of summer vacation helping Marija to receive the pilgrims and to go through and handle the mail which arrives from every part of the world. Only a few lines were needed to answer the most pitiable cases. It is incredible how many people turn to the Madonna in the various events of life. After a very intense and tiring week, Marija had left in the first afternoon for her spiritual exercises.

I decided to leave for Italy by night to avoid the humidity and the hot sun of the coast. I had some free time before me and I thought to go up into the room of the apparitions in Vicka's house. It is

Marija in the early days of the apparitions.

27

found, as those who frequently go to Medjugorje know, at the top of the stairs from which she usually transmits the messages of the Madonna to the people bunched up in the little court-yard. It was around four in the afternoon, and strangely there was no one around.

I entered the room where a beautiful life size statue of the Madonna held court while all around were gathered the objects which the pilgrims had brought for blessing. I knelt down and began to recite the rosary. A few minutes later I saw Vicka look in at the door. She had just returned from Zagreb where she had been hospitalized a few weeks before for an appendicitis operation. I barely knew her but I gathered my courage and asked her if she wanted to join in the recitation of the rosary. She agreed but remained standing because of her wound.

Around five o'clock, at the end of the rosary, all of a sudden I didn't hear her voice any more even though she was moving her lips. She had remained standing after having attempted to kneel. Her head was turned toward the ceiling. She smiling, talking, and nodding. She was talking to someone who was present in the little room and whom I did not see. I understood that the Madonna had arrived.

I felt a thud in my heart. I had no doubt that the Mother of God was at least 3 feet from me. I fell on my face to the ground, expressing my faith and professing my unworthiness. There were only the two of us in front of her. I was certain that on that occasion she was forced to see and listen to me. In that moment I had

Vicka during an apparition in the 1980's.

forgotten that the Madonna sees each of us in our uniqueness, even if we were as numerous as the sand on the seashore.

I told the Madonna everything that was in my heart, of the past, the present and the future of my life. I presented her many prayer intentions. I talked to her like a son turns to his mother. This kind of chance, I said to myself, would not happen to me again. Normally an apparition lasts a few minutes. After ten minutes I began to get restless. The apparition continued. Having finished my personal prayers I set about to take up the rosary again but was taken by curiosity to observe what was happening with an attentive eye.

Vicka was standing and looking lightly towards the sky. Later on she explained that the Madonna had said not to kneel because of her recent operation. The gentleness of Mary is moving. Her manner was absorbed and very lively at the same time. She was speaking with someone who inspired respect and trust. She was listening seriously, she nodded smilingly and she questioned with much involvement. On other occasions I have noticed that at the apparitions with Marija, Ivan and Ivanka to which I have been present, they speak more rarely and more calmly. Even in these particular moments the visionaries are themselves, each with his own personality.

The apparition lasted a little more than forty minutes. In all that time it was as if I didn't exist. Vicka did not direct her look to any other part not even for an instant; nor was she distracted by the usual house noises. She was as if immersed in another world. The ecstasy, if that is how we can call it, did not manifest unusual phenomena, if only a supernatural transfiguration of her face, particularly serene and full of light and a decorum of the whole person.

The only phenomenon completely outside of the ordinary was the disappearance of the voice. Vicka was talking in a more obvious way, so that you could hear the movement of the lips and of the tongue but you could not hear her voice. It was as if she had disappeared in the moment that the Madonna had arrived. In the first days of the apparitions on the Podbrdo, it was not like this. The people could hear the voices of the visionaries when they were talking to the Madonna.

In the succeeding apparitions their voices have totally disappeared while those present can see the movement of their lips. Evidently the Madonna wants to maintain her dialogues with the visionaries a secret but at the same time she leaves us a very significant sign of her presence. In fact who of us can speak normally without letting our voices be heard?

Suddenly, however, Vicka's voice could be clearly heard. Later on she told me that the Madonna had begun to pray the Our Father and Vicka was united with her saying "Who art in heaven..." Then quickly she prayed the Glory be to the Father. However, she did not recite the Hail Mary. As soon as those two prayers were finished, her voice disappeared again while the apparition continued.

I have been able to note that this phenomenon happens in all the apparitions of the Gospa. The voices of the visionaries, except for the first days, disappears at the beginning of the apparition. If they are praying, the moment the Madonna arrives, they immediately fall on their knees and their voices dissolve into nothing. It returns only when they pray the Our Father and the Glory Be with the Mother of God. To my knowledge, they have never said the Hail Mary, not even once. In fact, the Madonna does not pray to herself.

The phenomenon of the disappearance of the voice and its temporary return during the apparition is not to be underestimated. Under the scientific report, it poses some notable problems of interpretation. In fact the mouth and the tongue move as if they were speaking. Why can't we hear the voice? And why does it return during the prayer of the Our Father and the Glory Be to the Father, while the visionary is still in ecstasy? It seems that it is a sign that God leaves for us as proof of the authenticity of the apparition itself. It cannot be dismissed so superficially.

While I was writing this chapter, I had the opportunity to participate at an apparition of the visionary Marija in her home in Italy. It was the 7th of April, 1998, Tuesday in Holy Week. Many years have passed but nothing has changed from what I have described above. The context however is different. It makes a certain impression having the Madonna in your house while the water is boiling in the pot in the kitchen and the children are running here and there unaware of what is happening. The whole family was there: the parents, the three children, (the oldest of which was only four years old) and the grandparents. The Madonna, who enters into a domestic fireside, is an event full of significance.

After the rosary Marija starts to pray the seven Our Fathers, Hail Mary and Glory Be. The most lively child, Francesco Maria wants to play with his mom exactly when she is praying. Marija smiles and offers him a teddy bear there on the floor, trying to calm him down. Michael Maria, the eldest, succeeds in staying quiet for a few minutes. The youngest, Marco Maria, in the arms of his grandmother, observes the situation.

Near the end of the prayers the Madonna arrives. I think of this long faithfulness of the Mother of God with emotion, despite our apathy and superficiality. During the apparition Marija usually has a very serious expression which is impressive. It had never occurred to me to verify up to which point the ecstasy takes the visionary away from the external world. All of a sudden, the very lively Francesco Maria approaches his mom, attaches himself to her dress and calls her. Marija however does not move and does not take her eyes off where they are fixed on high. It seems as if she is neither seeing nor hearing the child. Even this detachment from the external world is a phenomenon which belongs to the signs of God.

The apparitions of the Madonna in Medjugorje are themselves a sign. In simplicity, in silence, in prayer, the supernatural enters into our dimension. Those present live the event in a climate of faith and peace. The visionaries see the Madonna with their eyes and God only knows what inexpressible joy fills their hearts in that moment. But those present, praying with their hearts, can have a similar experience because in the end all that matters is the intimate union of the soul with the world of God.

There is the moment when the Madonna leaves. I noticed Marija lowering her head and quickly afterwards saying the prayer of the Magnificat. Instead, Vicka emits a sound like a sigh, pronouncing the Croatian expression "Ode" which means "she is leaving," from the depths of her soul. Then there is a return to reality, very naturally. The visionaries, if asked and if it is necessary, give a very succinct report of the apparition.

I asked Vicka why there was an apparition of such length when the usual duration is a few minutes. She replied that the Madonna spoke to her of something which concerned her future. Later on I tried in vain to find out more. The visionaries of Medjugorje are very reserved. They testify the messages publicly, but in their private life try to live them more than talk about them. I have seen that Mary is moulding them in her image and likeness, teaching them to keep their experience closed in their hearts, giving them clear and loyal proof at the opportune time.

Many times I have asked how the youngsters will react and how will we react when this time of grace will end which through Mary "is united to heaven in a special way."

CHAPTER 4

I am your mother and I love you

THE MADONNA IS OUR MOTHER

"Tota Pulchra es Maria"; "You are beautiful, Mary" the Church sings along the course of the centuries from the time when the angel Gabriel, appearing to her in the moment of the Annunciation saluted her with the words, "full of grace." The pilgrims who come to Medjugorje listen willingly to the description of the beauty of the Madonna from the live voice of the visionaries. You see the eyes of the people bright with joy as if they were seeing something that no human imagination succeeds in representing.

One speaks very much of a totally supernatural beauty which rises from the depth of the soul full of God and that wraps in divine light all the human being of the Holy Mother. I had tried many times to imagine how the Madonna could seem based on the description of those

Our Lady as the seers most closely depict her.

who see her every day. This is a useless exercise, because it is a splendor of grace that the heart of each of us can only accept as a gift.

It is only recently that I have seemed to grasp the mystery of the being of Mary in her deepest roots, apart from the description that one can make with human words, always very poor and humble. I found myself at the vigil of the last day of 1997 in Medjugorje in a very beautiful little church in the middle of the woods just in front of the mountain of the first apparitions. It is the place of the prayers of the "Oasis of Peace," a Marian religious community, formed by young people of both sexes, born of the charism full of fervor of Fr. Gianni Sgreva.

The chapel was filled with people waiting for the rosary and the Holy Mass. That evening, those present had the grace to assist in the apparition of the Madonna to Marija who, when she comes to Medjugorje, lives nearby. The boys and girls of the "Oasis of Peace" are very charming. They are young people who come from every part of the world and who have found the love that has transformed their lives in Medjugorje.

They live very simply with whatever is donated to them or which they themselves produce by working. They dress in the colours grey and white with which the Madonna appears here. Father Gianni directs their many studies and they alternate prayer and work with receiving all those who are in need. I always see them happy, even in church, and this is for me a sure sign of good health both spiritually and mentally. Looking at them I am made aware that it is possible that the relationship between man and women can be lived as a sign of fraternity brotherhood and sincere friendship.

After the rosary and before the Holy Mass there is the highly evocative and unrepeatable moment of the apparition. There is always a great silence filled with emotion and of an elusive presence. At the end, Marija tells us that the Madonna has prayed over all those present and has blessed them, exhorting us not to forget that she is our mother and that she loves us.

"I am your mother and I love you." That evening these words entered my heart as if it was the first time that I had heard them. How many times in my catechesis had I explained that Jesus, before He died, had given us Mary as our Mother? How many times had I begged her like a son in the moment of need? And yet, never before then had that expression hit me, piercing my heart like a sharp sword of love and

pain; the love of the heart of Mary and the pain for our hearts which are so hard and slow to understand.

It was in that moment that the splendour of the beauty of Mary, how the visionaries of Medjugorje describe her, showed me its true significance. The face of light of Mary, the sweetness of her smile and the eternal youth of herself were those of a mother, indeed of my mother, the one given to me by God, the one whose heart loves, understands, accepts and comforts like no mother in the world has even been able to do or will be able to do until the end of time.

"What is the Madonna like?" the pilgrims ask, eager to know. Any words used to describe her would be cold and impersonal if they didn't capture the essence of Mary herself, the mother of us all. The Madonna reminds us of this innumerable times in her messages. She never tires repeating it and we can say that her goodness, her patience and compassion are almost infinite. These have lead her to ask God to allow her to remain such a long time with us, and we can only find an explanation in the infinite love of her maternal heart.

"No mother is a Mother like the Madonna" is repeated often by the visionaries. "She has all the most beautiful things," and even when she corrects, she does it with sweetness which penetrates and conquers the heart. She loves us like no one else in the world, except God. One could say, finally, that the maternal love of God arrives to us through her heart. Is it not wonderful that in those most particular moments, the Madonna exchanges a hug and a kiss with the visionaries, at a birthday or a name day or whenever there is need for tenderness and encouragement?

No one is outside the bounds of the maternal love of Mary. For her we are all important and many times she reminds us that she prays for each of us. Her heart is vigilant along every step of our way to sanctity, because she desires to bring us all to Paradise and she never ceases to love us even when we are far away from her and from her Son. She loves us so much that her heart cries tears of blood for each of us who becomes lost in sin.

Sometimes I think of the immense gift that Jesus has given us, entrusting us to Mary as our mother. It was His last thought, the extreme act of His love before dying on the cross. I also think of the great fiat of Mary for staying so long among us. Some say that in her messages she repeats herself. Don't earthly mothers repeat themselves? Don't they always give us the same advice even when we don't listen?

When children run blind and deaf toward the road to perdition, which mother would not speak? Who would not repeat ad infinitum the call towards salvation? Would anyone suggest that the Madonna be silent? Should a mother let her children be destroyed and lead astray by evil? In all the apparitions the Madonna shows herself as a mother. It seems to me however that in no place is there such an emphasis on her maternal goodness as in Medjugorje. In the most difficult situations, when the visionaries and their families were subjected to the stress of the special police, the youngsters during the apparitions would tell everything to the Madonna and she would listen attentively, "just like a confessor" because evidently she already knew about everything. In all this time she has followed them, has sustained them in the difficult moments, she has instructed them, has guided them and has formed them in the Christian virtues.

But Mary has done and is doing the same thing with each of us. She is a mother who doesn't exclude anyone. We are all noticed by her, in the most hidden fibres of our beings and she loves us all as if each of us were her only child. Understanding the maternal heart of Mary means to enter into the depths of her overflowing being of celestial beauty.

THE MADONNA IS ALIVE TODAY

The Madonna is not a symbol but is a living person today. It is a message of great explosive force for contemporary man. The fact that these people that I know and with whom I am talking, joking and eating have conversed one-on-one with a person who lived two thousand years ago has always struck me greatly and in some moments also comforted me. Who in fact doesn't have dark moments in life, in which Satan hurls darts inflamed with doubt against us, of anxiety, distress which overwhelm us without giving us rest? Who, even if believing, doesn't ask himself, like Job, about the mystery of evil and of death, fervently searching for rays of light when darkness attacks?

More than once I have found myself thinking that these people who had received all my trust were seeing the Madonna every day. Yes, the Madonna was there; therefore all of the Christian faith is true, from the first to the last word. If the Madonna is alive today, then the hereafter exists and human life has a destiny of glory. If the Madonna appears, that I am not alone and the little ship of my life does not sail without hope and without a goal. The idea that the Madonna is here, because some persons worthy of faith see her every day, represents a great strength and a reason to believe and of support for the faith that only a self conceited person could despise.

On some occasions I have heard criticisms about the importance that the simple people attribute to the visionaries. Certainly in Medjugorje charismatic figures have not been few who have attracted the interest of the pilgrims. Their words, however, even if very deep and passionate, have never been a substitute for the clear testimony of the visionaries that the Madonna is here and is alive today. The people understand that whoever has seen the Madonna carries a message of decisive importance. When one tells you that the Madonna exists, because he has seen her a few minutes ago, he gives you a much greater truth than a thousand sermons. An entire theological library would not have the same compelling value.

I remember an experience of a comic flavour that I lived in my first year of staying in Medjugorje. I was then helping Marjia to go through the mail and sometimes in welcoming the pilgrims whom she would receive on the stairs of her mother's house. It was in the times when the trips from Italy were beginning to increase. Marija had a very painful toothache and was not able to talk. She asked me to stay outside and receive the groups to give them some information and to help them recite some prayers.

In my enthusiasm as a beginner I would describe everything I had learned to the pilgrims: how the apparition occurred, how the Madonna showed herself, how were her clothes and I even gave information about heaven, hell and purgatory. The people listened willingly but when I let them understand that it was time to go to make space for other groups, nobody moved. "Now you know everything, what else do you want?" I would ask. "We want to see the seer," they would answer. They were right. Not I, but she was seeing the Madonna every day in the fullness of her person.

Some would say that faith is enough. Certainly! But when faith is lethargic, when it is exposed to doubt, when it is reduced to a smoking wick, when God seems silent, when this world seems to sink into disbelief, what light, what comfort, what strength it brings if a person gives you the certainty that the Madonna is here because he has seen her.

The witness of whoever sees the Madonna helps our faith. He verifies the existence of another world and confirms that everything in which he believes is real. The most important news that the youngsters give to the world for over 30 years of daily apparitions is that Mary, the Mother of Jesus is alive today.

MARY'S ETERNAL YOUTH

To describe what the Madonna is like is an almost impossible enterprise. Can human words represent a heavenly reality? Every time

the seers are invited to report the particulars about how the Mother of God looks, they clearly find themselves in difficulty. They repeat to the point of boredom that there are no words that can describe what they see and hear. Saint Paul is the first to warn us that the hereafter is indescribable. From then, all who have that experience are in agreement in saying that words capable of expressing it do not exist.

It needs to be said that the apparition is a grace. Not only in the sense that those to whom the Madonna shows herself have received a very particular gift, but also in the sense that to be able to see the Madonna and talk to her, a special grace is necessary... a grace that fortifies and elevates our fragile and weak human nature. Our poor mortal eyes cannot even look at the light of the sun or at the light from a very bright lamp. How can we look at the Mother of God in the radiance of her celestial beauty, which reflects in herself the splendour of the risen Christ?

A special grace allows the seers to enter the supernatural world enfolded by divine glory, which is inaccessible and unbearable by human nature alone. We need to be very careful not to depict Our Lady as merely human. Many pilgrims display innocence and elicit tenderness when they show the seers this or that photograph of the Madonna wishing to confirm that she looks like the image in the picture.

The supernatural is not of this world. It is something totally different and infinitely greater. The supernatural is awe-inspiring, sublime, inexpressible. At times it leaves signs in our visible sphere; but these signs in their simplicity, full of purity and light, take us quickly to something higher.

No one can flatter himself to represent the Madonna after he has heard the visionaries' description. Mary is a being of light. She is the woman clothed in the sun that is penetrated by the dazzling splendour of God. All her person, soul and body are part of the divine glory that radiates from the risen Christ. In her the Blessed Trinity has taken up residence, becoming, in St. Louis de Montfort's expression, 'the Paradise of God.'

After Jesus, who by means of the mystery of the Incarnation has become "the most beautiful in all humanity," no beauty can be compared to that of Mary. Hers is the saved human condition, elevated and transfigured by grace. She is the human being who participates perfectly with divine nature.

When the visionaries are in conversation with Mary, you, in some way see the reflection of the divine world by which they are enraptured. Their faces are lightly transfigured and their whole person emanates composure, concentration and serenity. It has happened for me on more than one occasion to speak to them immediately after the apparition. The passage from the supernatural experience to the daily dimension is fairly rapid. Nevertheless you perceive in them a great peace and deep joy which according to the visionary Marija fill the heart even in the case of seeing the Madonna sad or even crying. The eyes of each of them, especially after the apparition are full of a particular light.

What affects the visionaries before all is the divine beauty of Mary. It is a beauty that is not of this world. It is the splendour of a soul filled with God which surrounds and transfigures the body. The Madonna has a real body but not like ours, still subject to the wear and tear of time that passes, to the heaviness of matter and the sting of sickness and death, but transfigured, spiritualized and sanctified. Mary, so says our faith, foresees in herself the destiny of all who are saved, who at the end of time will participate in the glory of the resurrection of Christ.

Her beauty is celestial harmony, splendour of grace and eternal youth. When the Madonna appears, her body is wrapped in light and her attitude is that of prayer. She comes from God and as soon as she comes in contact with our world, she quickly leads us back to God. The apparition for all those present is immersion in the universe of prayer and of peace. When she arrives, the seers fall on their knees. The human world, difficult, wasted, and afflicted by the many torments of life is elevated to the divine sphere.

The visionaries are in agreement in declaring that the Madonna appears like a young woman of about 20 years old. Maybe it is the age when she, on this earth, who was greeted from heaven as "Full of grace," opened her soul and her womb to the mystery of the Incarnation. Her perpetual youth testifies for eternity the unique and unrepeatable instant in which the word is made flesh and the divine nature is married to the human nature. Her age will always be the age in which she became the *Theotokos*, the Mother of God and at the same time, our Mother.

What do the eyes of the Madonna look like? Her hair? Her voice? The questions are never-ending especially by the Italian pilgrims who, since almost all of them have a picture of the Madonna in their homes, hope that theirs will be the one which resembles her. Personally I have always retained that these questions are pertinent and even intelligent. I have always been careful of snobbery. In fact they put in plain words, in their own way, the realism of the faith in the resurrection in which the Virgin Mary who was assumed into heaven already shares.

The eyes of the Madonna are real eyes, blue in colour, in which the depth of her spirituality is mirrored. Her gaze penetrates to the roots of the soul. There is no need for the Madonna to scold because all is understood in her look. What affects the visionaries the most is the tone of her voice that they are unable to describe. It almost seems as if she is singing. They say, "It is a sweet voice, very youthful, but at the same time very serious. Her voice is so deep that we are unable to describe its beauty. We can say that at the same time it is like music because if you are not feeling well inside, on hearing the Madonna, you are healed."

The face of Mary expresses the state of her soul, as it happens to us, even if she never loses the divine splendour of her beauty. The Madonna often smiles and even laughs. Once she also cried with real tears. Often I have heard the pilgrims ask, "Is the Madonna happy today?" Do these questions make any sense? I believe they do even if the reasons of happiness and of pain of the Mother of God are very different from our own. The Madonna is full of joy if her children are walking the road of sainthood, while she is sad if they become lost in sin.

The shock of the visionary Marija was notable on June 26th, 1981. After the apparition on Podbrdo, while she was returning home along a steep path, the Madonna appeared to her again and was weeping real tears. Behind her was a cross without the crucified Christ. The tears were falling down onto her dress and were being lost on the cloud on which the she was standing. The tears of the Madonna invited mankind to peace, first with God and then among themselves. Marija was very moved seeing the Blessed Mother crying, and she who was so shy ran quickly to give the message to people so that the Madonna would be consoled.

Exactly ten years after this, the 26th of June, 1991 the war which sowed pain and death in all of former Yugoslavia exploded. This caused the kind of destruction with casualties not seen in Europe since the Second World War.

Perhaps you may ask yourselves why the Madonna does not smile or laugh. Naturally her laugh is not abundant in the world. The laugh which flowers in Paradise cannot be but the expression of divine joy of which hearts are overflowing. Perhaps you can allow me to retell a personal testimony about the laugh of the Madonna.

Once I had the grace to be present at an apparition of the Madonna with Vicka in a little room in her birth house. With me were Vicka's sister, Anna and another person. Anna and I asked Vicka if she could ask the Madonna to give us the grace to become saints. It was in the first times when I was going to Medjugorje, for which you will forgive me these excesses of presumption. Vicka was more or less perplexed but then she agreed. Probably for her, a young girl who is very simple and humble, these requests seemed too bold. She told us to kneel down beside her, one on her left and one on her right. During the apparition I became aware that Vicka had asked the Madonna the question because moving her head first on one side and then on the other, she was indicating Anna and me.

At the end of the apparition I did not dare ask anything. I feared a reply which implied a pulling of the ears. Instead, Vicka herself very surprised, told us that at her request the Madonna had started to laugh with joy. Just like that! I understood that nothing can make the Madonna so happy than the commitment of her small children to proceed along the walk of sanctity holding her hand.

Without ever losing her profound peace, the Madonna expresses sentiments similar to ours. Sometimes she is serious and other times she is happy. She smiles, laughs and even cries. It is her motherly love and the events of our souls that influence her state of mind and the outline of her features.

How the Madonna appears is also defined by outward signs which are very significant even if not always understandable. The grey dress and the white veil are perhaps an invitation to repentance and to purity of life. The twelve stars surrounding her head "among themselves unbound but alive and which give the Madonna a supernatural beauty" (Marija) and the cloud under her feet indicate her dignity and her greatness as Queen of heaven and earth. Also the regal character of the Queen of Peace is emphasized from the splendour of her vestments on the occasions of the great feast days. In fact the Psalm speaks of her when it affirms, "The daughter of the King is all splendour, gems and of golden threads is her dress." (Psalm 45)

It is therefore the Mother and the Queen who appears in Medjugorje. It is the Madonna that the Church venerates. She is a celestial person but profoundly human at the same time. She allows herself to be proclaimed on earth by three lamps of light, to indicate that she comes from heaven. She returns to heaven absorbed in prayer, leaving in her wake the symbols of the cross, of the heart and of the sun whose significance cannot escape the attentive contemplation. The cross indicates the price with which we have been redeemed. The heart reveals the infinite love of the hearts of Jesus and Mary. The sun is God himself, toward whom we must turn like the flowers in the morning to receive light, heat and life.

There is no doubt that the first and most important message of Medjugorje is the existence of the Madonna herself, clothed in the splendour of the glory of heaven, but a Mother forever. It is she who takes an interest in each one of us, loving us with a love which if we would comprehend, would make us cry with joy.

CHAPTER 5

God has sent me to you because of love

THE MADONNA REVEALS HERSELF IN HER MESSAGES

There is no doubt that the description of the Madonna in the mystery of her person, in the way she is presented to us by the visionaries of Medjugorje, corresponds perfectly to the teaching of the faith. Mary is Queen of Heaven and earth, the Mother of God and our own, to whose maternal heart Jesus has entrusted us. In the splendour of her beauty she is 'full of grace', taken body and soul in the Assumption into the divine glory of heaven. Can we be surprised then, that after an extraordinarily long time, the visionaries are still not tired of meeting her every day, but in fact, wait for this moment with great interior joy?

The world of the supernatural is rich in mystery, with its own reality which is always new and full of promise. Evil, on the other hand, is repetitive and enslaves to itself with its monotonous and hopeless rhythms. I am very much struck by the way in which Ivanka lives her experience of encountering the Madonna only once a year, on the 25th

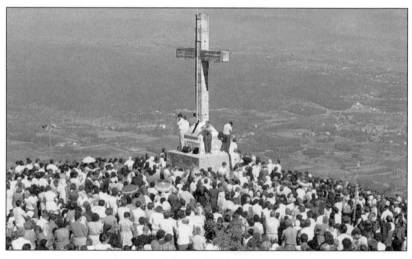

Mount Krizevac

of June, the day of the anniversary of the first apparition. I had gone to her since I had little hope of finding any space during the anniversary when many pilgrims would be there.

I arrived when the dining room of her house was already packed with people and I had to be content to observe from the doorway. In a certain sense it was an advantage because I could see Ivanka up close when she entered and exited. As soon as the apparition started, something unusual happened. Ivanka turned to those present, asking them to kneel. Only in the first days of the apparitions could the visionaries in the moments of ecstasy be in contact with the world surrounding them. Evidently the Madonna had noticed that in the people surrounding them there was a climate more of curiosity than of prayer.

Ivanka passed in front of me, very happily waiting for the great event. The expression on her face remained very absorbed and serene through the entire apparition except for one moment in which a cloud of dismay seemed to darken it. At the end, turning to those present among which I noted René Laurentin with his notebook, Ivanka said that the Madonna had shown her a scene of great suffering, which was impossible to describe. She said nothing else. I saw her walk in front of me in tears, her face showing great pain. A shiver passed through me from head to toe. What was it about? What was waiting for us? All those present were asking themselves and were exchanging opinions. I was thinking again about Ivanka's face and was asking myself what tremendous message she had received. I later learned that the reason for her tears was not about what the Madonna had shown her but the fact that she would not see her for another year.

These experiences of the visionaries find a satisfactory explanation only in the contacts with the supernatural. For them it is like entering into the light of Paradise. The vision of Mary in her infinite beauty and maternal goodness confirm what the faith teaches about the Madonna. They can experience a relationship of childlike love which the Marian doctrines illustrate with rigorous theological language.

Some people, superficially and without respect, say that the Madonna in Medjugorje talks too much. In truth her messages can be gathered in a booklet. It cannot be said that there are many who think that these messages contain a magisterial authority that has lasted many years. Every word which comes out of the mouth of Mary is to be received like a great grace and seen in the light of the Holy Spirit. The

Madonna at Medjugorje, as in other Marian apparitions, comes first of all to pray.

Nevertheless, the messages that until now Mary has given in Medjugorje allow us by means of a fully respectful examination to understand how the Madonna presents herself and what role she intends to develop. By means of these we can verify if her way of being and acting correspond to the teachings of the faith. In this analysis, it must be said that rarely have the writings about Mary been able to present the Mother of God in her role of Handmaid of the Lord. Also rarely have they presented her as Mother of the Church and of humanity with the depth and the existential strength which emerge from the messages of Medjugorje.

In these messages, a totally passionate love for God and a zeal so fervent for His glory and the eternal salvation of souls is manifested, that they indicate a spiritual greatness which goes to the farthest end of our understanding. When a person speaks, he inevitably manifests who he is. The rivers of messages which are now in circulation, some gathered in large volumes are in large part of such an average spiritual profile that just for this they cannot be attributed to the Madonna or to Jesus.

Overflow Mass crowd behind St. James Church.

The Madonna in Medjugorje speaks like a Madonna. Hers are the words of she who is the Seat of Wisdom, the Wise Virgin, the Mother and the Teacher of the people of God. In my opinion, today no one speaks of God like the Madonna in Medjugorje. No one demonstrates a similar zeal for the salvation of the world. No one gives us knowledge so magnificent, be it only through a sober and simple language, about prayer, about the journey of sanctity, and about eternal life. The messages of Medjugorje are the most beautiful comment that is written today on the Gospel of Jesus.

Now the task is to understand first of all what role the Virgin assigns herself in the divine plan of redemption which is being realized in our times.

THE ONE SENT BY GOD TO CONTEMPORARY MAN

In her most profound humility, the Madonna has not hesitated to define herself as the Handmaid of the Lord. She is this not only in the moment of the Annunciation, but always in time and in eternity. Mary is the Eternal Handmaid, she who is in every moment at the service of God. This is how the Madonna presents herself in Medjugorje. What strikes us in this appearance of the supernatural is that not only are the visionaries and the parish but also the Madonna 'instruments' at the service of a design of love born from God's heart.

On various occasions the Queen of Peace asserts that she has been sent by God. She does not come on her own initiative, as if she wants to put herself in first place. She is "sent" and her coming among us is at the same time an act of obedience to God and for love of man. Even the plan that she is leading and bringing to completion what she started at Fatima belongs to the divine designs. The messages, in particular that of peace, are entrusted to her by God himself.

Undoubtedly, the Madonna acts and takes initiatives in the first person and does not hesitate to speak also of her plans and of her messages, but this is only to indicate her perfect devotion to the will of her Lord. When once, because of the apathy of the parish, she warned that she may not give any more messages, she very significantly added, "*God is permitting me that.*" (Feb. 21/85)

She invites the parishioners to fast in order to thank God for allowing her to remain such a long time. (Sept.20/84) It is God himself, in fact, who allows her to remain with us to teach us and to help us to find the path to peace. (March 25/88) When she decides to give the messages not every Thursday but every 25th of the month, the Madonna gives us a reason saying that *"The time has come when what my Lord desired has been fulfilled."* (Jan. 8/87)

The Madonna does not attract attention to herself nor does she allow her person to be the aim of those who rush to her. She comes in the name of God to show us His love and to bring us back to Him. From the messages of Medjugorje, the Madonna appears as the instrument with which the infinite love of God for man manifests itself and which has never happened before in the Christian story.

Mary is sent in mission to a world over which *"sin dominates," "a new world without God"* that man wants to build with his own power. In the messages of Medjugorje there are neither catastrophic signs nor any gloomy or distressing language such as appear in other supposed private revelations. Nevertheless the spiritual situation of contemporary man is described with masterstrokes of valuable realism; man is he who aspires to total liberation from God to become absolute master of his own life.

In this image of great danger for humanity, the mercy of God which does not want to abandon man to himself is manifested. Here is God who sends His messenger after a century of darkness and death and a humanity facing a future which looks even darker due to its stubbornness on the road of evil. Who better than Mary could He have sent? Who, if not she, could prepare the return of the world to its Creator? The duration of the apparitions, the number and the intensity of the messages and the universal scope of the summons indicate that we are facing a divine intervention without precedent.

In these first two Christian millennia the Madonna has come to earth numerous times. God has sent her to help, recall and sustain the Christian people in particular situations. We do not exactly know what Mary's statement means when she says that her appearances in Medjugorje will be the last Marian apparitions on earth. This is confirmed by all the visionaries. But one has the impression that here we are facing something unique and different compared to the past.

Facing one of the most important turning points in history, before a decisive crossroad where man could enter the road of death, here is the exceptional answer, proportional to the danger: *"God sends me to you out of love, that I may help you to comprehend that without Him there is no future or joy and, above all, there is no eternal salvation."* (April 25/97)

The Madonna in Medjugorje shows herself as she who is sent from heaven for the fulfilment of a mission of salvation of epic proportions. Having been entrusted a task from on high, she has laid her hand to a job whose greatness manifests itself with always increasing clarity.

ALL THE MESSAGES CRY OUT: "GOD!"

The Madonna in the Medjugorje messages speaks tirelessly of God. The themes which she touches perhaps are not popular among a large part of the preachers but they are of a pure evangelical mold. Sent by God she proposes to help contemporary man who has lost the transcendent dimension of life. She is to help man rediscover God and with Him the way of peace, of joy and salvation. The lesson of Mary is the most luminous example of what is the "new evangelization."

Looking at her, the Church can understand always more profoundly the fundamentals of her mission which is bringing souls to heaven. Was the Church founded for other reasons? In the messages of Medjugorje there is a return to the essential elements of the faith and of Christian life that in the short period of the century were as if extinguished.

It would now be too easy to open an argument against a certain kind of Christianity which with the excuse of being popular in the world has ended up losing itself. However it is not necessary to surrender to the temptation to present the apparitions of Medjugorje as a bulwark of "traditionalism." The Madonna evades these pitiful ideas. She

Medjugorje means 'between the mountains.'

47

reminds the world and the Church of something absolute that cannot be denied: faith, grace, prayer, the sacraments, the sanctity of life, the vision of eternity. She reminds us of the primacy of prayer, the unquestionable necessity of conversion, the detachment of the heart from sin to live, even on this earth, with hearts overflowing with the joy of God.

Her invitations are simple but they always go to the heart of things. The cross, the Eucharist, the Mass, confession, the reading of the bible, Eucharistic adoration, the rosary are all central to her maternal call. But what is most urgent for her is prayer. There is not a message which does not contain a direct or indirect invitation to prayer. For what reason? In fact it is thanks to prayer that man can find God and experience Him in his life.

Is this it? I ask myself whether there is anything more important than taking a generation which risks losing Him, back to God. I ask if there is something more essential in Christianity than the mystery of the cross and the Eucharist. I ask: is prayer not the starting point of a Christian life? The Madonna in Medjugorje proposes to bring the Church sweetly but firmly back to the heart of its mystery.

I must say that for me, a priest, certain apparently obvious messages have touched my heart initiating a debate. Who of us hasn't felt himself shaken and personally reminded when the Madonna has said *"Put God in the first place"* or *"Abandon yourselves completely to God"* or *"Decide for God."* We believed that we had already made our choices but we discovered that our belonging to God was only formal where in fact we were living as if He didn't exist.

What a new universe opened up when I – coming from a plethora of readings and who believed that I knew enough – would hear the Madonna invite us to *"find God the creator in prayer"* and *"discover Him in the smallest flower."* What consolation for everyone but especially for those away from Him, hearing from the mouth of the Madonna that God never abandons us. Even when we are far away from Him, He continues to love us and *"gives us the possibility for conversion every day."*

What a mistake to think that the Madonna places herself at the attention of the faithful! From the messages of Medjugorje the primacy of God over life emerges with the same intensity as the light of the sun. In Mary's school we learn to search for Him, above all in prayer, to find Him in the activities of daily life and to thank Him for all that He gives us every day, to entrust our existence and everything we possess to Him, and to serve Him by cooperating in His plan of salvation.

The Madonna wants to bring us to such a deep familiarity with God in a particular way so that we can live a real and proper bond of friendship with Him. In fact, *"Open your heart and give time to God so that He will be your friend. When true friendship with God is realized, no storm can destroy it."* (June 25/97) The insistent invitations to live the Holy Mass and to dedicate time to Eucharistic adoration are to help us become friends of Jesus. In that way *"you will not talk of Him like someone whom you barely know."* (Sept. 9/95) Mary wants to lead us to this intimacy with God, into the same intimacy in which she lives and which fills her with infinite joy.

I AM THE MEDIATRIX BETWEEN YOU AND GOD

There is an assertion by the Madonna that could explain very complex theological discussions. In a message she announces that she is the Mediatrix between us and God. But is not Jesus Christ the only mediator? There is no doubt that only the Incarnate Word is the way which leads to the Father. Only He who is God-made-man gives God to man and man to God. The Madonna however is between us and Jesus. Her mediation consists in standing by Jesus until the end of time in the work of salvation.

In a difficult moment for the Church and for the future of mankind, who could Jesus send us than she who by his divine decision is the Mother of the Church and of humanity? *"I am calling you to reflect upon why I am with you this long. I am the Mediatrix between you and God."* (July 17/86) To help us understand what her mission consists of, the Madonna often resorts to the image of flowers: *"Children, I wish to make of you a most beautiful bouquet prepared for eternity."* (July 25/95)

Mary's mission is solidified in this amazing image. She is invited by God to reawaken in us the lost and sleeping faith, to help us find again the sense, the beauty and the greatness of life and finally *"to save all souls and present them to God."* (Aug. 25/91) This is her desire, for this she has come and invites us to pray so that what she began at Fatima could be completely realized.

Undoubtedly the Madonna attracts us to herself. The visionaries themselves do not hesitate to confirm that especially at first, they were as if: "in love with Mary." Then slowly they opened themselves to all the greatness of the Christian mystery: "We have grown spiritually along with Mary...we have in a certain sense fallen in love with her. Especially at the beginning, I don't say that we were dependent, nevertheless the beauty of her face and her voice when she spoke drew us to her ...Then slowly she brought us to Jesus, toward the Church, to the Eucharist and she helped us to discover a world so great, so immense..."[3]

Who of those who have let themselves be guided by Mary to Medjugorje could not say the same thing? Mary attracts us to her but she doesn't hold us back. She dresses us in her beauty and she prepares us for eternity. Even the theme of the consecration to her heart, which is mentioned here and there, is based on a radically Christological outlook: *"I am inviting you to consecration to my Immaculate Heart. I want you to consecrate yourselves as parents, as families and as parishioners so that all belong to God through my heart."* (Oct. 25/88) Her desire is that through her heart, all our hearts belong to the heart of Jesus.

I would like to conclude these reflections referring to a sensation that I have often felt in my trips to Medjugorje. There, in Mary's parish, where she has appeared daily for such a long time, one almost always feels immersed in the mystery of the Eucharist. The Holy Mass and Eucharistic adoration, not the apparition, are the strongest moments in this earthly parish. The meeting with Mary produces in almost all the pilgrims the reawakening of faith, the desire for conversion, the searching of the confessional and the beginning of a new life with God.

She calls men and women from every part of the world to this holy place as well as many young people, who often have no more reasons to live. With her they rediscover God and the meaning of living. With her they find the Way, the Truth and the Life. With her they meet Jesus and through Him joy and peace. To today's lost, tormented humanity, prisoner of evil, Mary says: *"God sends me to help you and to guide you towards paradise, which is your goal."* (Sept. 25/94)

CHAPTER 6

Thank you for having responded to my call

MARY CALLS EACH ONE PERSONALLY

Medjugorje is a worldwide phenomenon. But it does not have many characteristics of it. We Italians, even if we are one of the closest countries, have had the sensation of making an endless journey even from the beginning. I ask myself: what do those who come from America, from Africa, from Asia or from the various countries of Eastern Europe think of this? Whoever sets out to answer the invitation of the Madonna needs to enter into the attitude of a pilgrim which permits few if any of the demands of tourism. Going to Medjugorje is a sacrifice. It is so especially today when the interior joy cancels fatigue and hardships.

As well, I ask myself, with all the news of apparitions which come from every part of the globe, how did this small and unknown village, then under the communist yoke, place itself at the centre of world attention? From 1985 I have spent my annual holiday month there helping Marija and then Vicka in receiving the pilgrims. I have been able to see with my own eyes a bursting river increasing from year to year involving persons from every race, language and nation.

The Church even today does not allow official pilgrimages. This means that the pilgrims do not contact those centres of assembly which are the parishes and the dioceses and not even those powerful organizations of religious tourism. Even the propaganda of the mass media has not been able to be affected. The communist regime for its part was doing its best to discredit, discourage and obstruct. The local bishop was asking for episcopal solidarity to discourage the faithful particularly from the European bishops. In Italy, mass media among the most circulated in the Catholic world also came onto the field to block the influx of pilgrims.

Humanly speaking, the phenomenon should have been suffocated at birth. But the more that water was thrown onto the fire, the more the fire flared up. People were organizing themselves. Persons of good will would spring up and were suddenly setting up travel agencies from the most unlikely places. In Medjugorje the farmers were quickly adapting to leaving their fields to dedicate themselves to receiving the people. In a short time a net of communication formed which now has planetary dimensions.

The drum beat of those devoted to the Gospa has been unstoppable. Whoever was in Medjugorje in the first years and returns now asks himself who is it that is gathering men and women in that village, among which are many youths from every part of the world. If you ask those who come whether it is a black, white or yellow face, he'll tell you that he has come because the Madonna called him. This is in fact the mysterious experience of numerous pilgrims and that in a certain sense distinguishes Medjugorje from other places of pilgrimage.

There are many possibilities for pilgrimages at the disposal of the faithful today. Whoever leafs through the glossy travel agency pamphlets will find before him, to say the least, a planetary offer. All the prominent shrines of the world are objects of organized trips. There are many people who having worked all their lives, take the satisfaction of a beautiful trip to a place honoured by popular devotion. It is undoubtedly a positive phenomenon. Medjugorje however has something profoundly different.

A person who feels called interiorly comes here. How? In the most unthinkable and unexpected ways. At times pilgrims arrive from so far away that they can't even say themselves how or why they have come. Having had the same experience myself, I have never had any difficulty in believing those of others. Some perhaps might ask if it is not an illusion. Is it possible that the Madonna is calling us one by one?

It really seems that way. Indeed it is certainly that way because in another way we cannot understand why at the end of each message she says, "*Thank you for having responded to my call.*" Mary personally calls the pilgrims to Medjugorje. To feel ourselves in the rays of her maternal concern imparts a joy which gives us wings despite the fatigue and the difficulty of the voyage.

THE THIRSTY FOR THE ABSOLUTE

What is special about Medjugorje? Are shrines like Lourdes, Fatima or La Salette not consecrated by the presence of Mary? I have often heard Vicka explain to the pilgrims that the Madonna in Medjugorje is alive, in the sense of her daily arrival from heaven to earth. It's a very important clarification. Not to detract anything from the other shrines where Mary has appeared in the past, but it is important to grasp God's moment, that is the hour in which the Divine Mercy operates. The apparitions of Medjugorje are today's time and place of a great blessing.

The Madonna states this many times saying that this is the time of great grace for the world. She reprimands us more than once for not being conscious of it and of letting it pass without results. *"Now you do not comprehend this grace, but soon a time will come when you will lament for these messages."* (Aug. 25/97) The people, even unconsciously, notice that heaven offers a unique opportunity which will not return again.

It is not possible to underestimate the coming of Mary on earth. She is the one sent by God, the messenger of an extravagant design of love. It is not a small thing that Mary comes every day to pray with and for us. Which generation like ours has had the immeasurable grace to have her as a teacher of spiritual life and as a guide on the road to sanctity? This is because of her messages, so simple but at the same time so full of divine wisdom. Who has ever had the grace, like the pilgrims of Medjugorje, to receive her maternal benediction?

I think about certain starry nights on Podbrdo or near the Blue Cross when thousands of people were crouched among the rocks, present at the apparition, the Madonna stretching her hand urging all to prayer and conversion. Then she would leave giving the blessing of peace and joy. You would see these people returning to the flatland, slipping through the thorny bushes and sliding on sharp stones, singing songs of jubilation while the sky above seemed so near, so populated, so friendly.

These are unique and unrepeatable experiences which no generation has ever had and that in no other part of the earth is possible. You would see the mothers and the grandmothers with faces hollowed out with fatigue but full of faith. You would see mature men with tearful eyes. You would see above all young people many of which had arrived in Medjugorje like stray dogs, at the margins of life, but who felt the tenderness of Mary landing on the arid and thirsty land of their hearts. Many found themselves there after a long wandering, with nothing left, like the Son of Man without even a rock on which to lay His head.

Those thirsty for the Absolute come to Medjugorje from every part of the world. They come with their burdens, their sorrows, their fears and their hopes. The defeated of society arrive there, the ill, the restless, the desperate. The satiated of the earth, those who now are laughing, those who are under the illusion that life is made safe with things, those who are well set up in the seductive niches of power and honour do not feel the need for Medjugorje. But all the rest, the hungry and thirsting for eternity, perceive an irresistible attraction.

Mary attracts, Mary fascinates, Mary calls. It would not be right to place limits in the actions of the Divine Mercy which operates everywhere in the world with supreme liberty. The places of grace are infinite. But in Medjugorje there is that special grace of being the chosen place of divine benediction in this new millennium. There Mary is alive and acts like in nowhere else in the world.

It is incredible with what wise direction the Madonna has worked. People have come in successive waves which seemed to be directed by heaven. In the very first days the Croatian pilgrims came by the thousands. Shortly after the waves of Italians turned up, followed by the French, the Germans, the Irish, the Belgians, the Swiss. Then it was the turn of the Americans whose multitudes populated Medjugorje till the eve of the war.

When the violence exploded, how many mouths were fed, how many wounds were treated, how many tears were dried from the solidarity of those who had previously received much on the spiritual level. The Italians, it is right to recognize, were the most generous on the level of helping and for this they have received special blessings for their country from the Madonna.

After the war it was the turn of the pilgrims from Eastern Europe, the Polish, the Czechs, and the Slovaks. The Hungarians were added to the others making of Medjugorje a world-wide parish, where the Christians rediscover the zeal of the faith, the sweetness of prayer and most of all the ultimate reasons for life. An immeasurable crowd of seekers of God have found each other in this unknown village of Herzegovina as in no other part of the world. It is there that Mary is moulding the Church for the third millennium.

THE TEARS OF JOY

What do the pilgrims do in Medjugorje? They pray. It is impossible to do anything else. Medjugorje is the largest centre of prayer in the world. Could it be any different in Mary's parish? There people discover the simplest way, the most essential and the most necessary way to be a Church: to pray. Perhaps we had forgotten it. Maybe in our parishes prayer has slowly passed into the second place. Maybe in the same church it is not so clear that *"nothing is more important than prayer."*

In Medjugorje, prayer beats like a heart inflamed with love first of all in the parish church where all day holy Masses and rosaries follow each other one after the other in the various languages of the world. But then it overflows outside the walls of the church and of the various chapels to invade the roads, the piazzas, the fields, the hills and the same celestial vault which covers the immense clearing like an infinitely spacious temple.

In Medjugorje prayer is like the air one breathes. You see groups with the rosary in their hands while they cross the paths through the fields which bring you to the hill of the first apparitions or to the mountain of the cross. Even the visits to the houses of the visionaries have the characteristics of a pilgrimage, where the songs, the moments of silence and the chants beat the time of the proceedings slowly and solemnly. It has happened to me sometimes to climb Podbrdo in the early morning and to find dispersed among the rocks, facing the cross, immovable figures, as if sculptured in the rock, captivated in a mysterious and indescribable encounter.

When you enter this strip of land kissed by heaven, a secret joy, an unknown peace knocks at the door of your heart. Who can know the sensational victories of grace in hardened hearts, lacerated by evil, menaced by doubt and by desperation? What jubilation and feasting every day in heaven for the tears of repentance and of the joy which descend silently and unceasingly through the faces of those arriving in Medjugorje searching for God.

While the people pray, Mary works silently in hearts. She has said many times that in this place of divine predilection she grants particular graces; first of all that of reawakening our faith and changing our lives. Mary prays for each one of us and intercedes constantly so that our hearts accept the tremendous gift of conversion. You see its fruit in the incessant lines of the faithful who patiently wait their turn in front of the confessionals which surround the parish church on the outside.

In our parishes the confessionals are barely used both by the priests or the faithful. In some parts they have become an archeological exhibit. I remember being touched but also saddened when I went to visit the little church of Ars and I stopped in front of the confessional of the Holy Saint Curé. It was there, abandoned, like an object from another time. The confessionals in Medjugorje are as crowded as are the bars or supermarkets at home. The people seal the encounter with Mary by asking pardon of Jesus for their sins and beginning a new life according to the commandments of God.

In Mary's parish conversion is a reality which you can touch with your hands. People arrive there who you would never have expected. How many, kept away from the church by prejudices, by arguments, by ideologies, by scandals, by indifference, by grudges, are softened and abandon themselves like babies in the arms of their Mother! How many lives devastated by vice are reconstructed! Even young people destroyed by drugs have started a new life in Medjugorje. In the "Camp of Life" of Sister Elvira you see what resurrections the Madonna is able to accomplish.

Medjugorje is outside of the normal geography of religious tourism. Without taking anything away from the other Marian shrines, locations famous for popular piety and Marian dedication, this place has something unique and extraordinary. Whoever arrives there is very quickly aware of it. People go home from Medjugorje transformed.

THE MESSENGERS OF PEACE

Medjugorje has many friends, especially among the simple people, but even from among hardened enemies. Unfortunately, in the pure light of the things of God creeps the weakness of human dust in its selfishness and pride. It has always been thus from the dawning of redemption. God knows mankind better than anyone but evidently He has decided to support him with His infinite patience, using him for His plans, in spite of the damage man can cause.

The accusations directed at the followers of the Gospa in the course of the years have not stuck, like mud that is thrown which dries and dissolves without leaving a trace. One of these objectives was of attributing to the pilgrims an excessive search for heavenly signs. The crowds who were rushing in with great sacrifices from every part of the world and who received the messages of prayer and conversion with great seriousness were supposed to be driven by false and superstitious motivations.

In truth the Madonna at first left some visible signs of her presence. Even in other apparitions she acted in the same way. Is the water which begins to spring forth at the foot of the grotto of Lourdes and the miracle of the sun at Fatima not perhaps a sign? The citizens of Medjugorje were comforted by some extraordinary signs especially in the first months, when the repression had characteristics of police-state persecution.

The most significant sign is the writing of the word 'MIR' (peace) which appeared in the sky in letters of fire for all the inhabitants to see. Many also relate about the disappearance of the cross on Mt. Krizevac substituted for some minutes by the statue of the Madonna. Others also testify about the setting sun which in some occasions took the form of a large white host surrounded by fire. Not to mention the hundreds of extraordinary healings testified to at the parish office.

Mount Krizevac

All of this, however, acts like dressing for an event more significant and essential, which is the re-awakening of the faith at the beginning of the walk of conversion. This goes for the parish as well as for the pilgrims who arrive there. In Medjugorje there is a climate of prayer and moral and spiritual renaissance which I personally have not met anywhere else.

The sincerity of the pilgrims has always impressed me. From the top of the stairs at Vicka's house I have seen them pass in the tens of thousands. It was like all the parishes of the world in procession. For me it has been an extraordinary ecclesial experience; faces attentive, intense, reflective, marked by life but open to hope. They want to know what the Madonna is asking of them. They listen attentively, moved with thankfulness and they go with hearts overflowing with a secret joy. They have the confirmation that the Madonna is there, that she loves them, that she protects them and she accompanies them on the road toward heaven.

Wherever grace touches, the fruits are quick to manifest themselves. The changing of lives is the biggest miracle which can happen on earth. The healing of the sick, the resurrection of the dead or the movement of mountains do not impress me as much as a conversion. The greatest event that can happen to man, the most extraordinary manifestation of the power of God, is the transformation of a heart which is a prisoner of sin.

The people who go home from Medjugorje in the great majority of the cases are different from the ones who left for the journey. Something elusive has struck them. And yet, humanly speaking, in Medjugorje there is nothing extraordinary. The whole picture is rather humble. The discomforts are not few. Many do not even have the small joy of meeting the visionaries or to have an external sign of the divine presence.

Something happens in the heart in a mysterious and secret way. You see people who return happy, full of enthusiasm and holy intentions. Many enter into prayer groups, others begin to participate in parish activities, becoming the messengers of that divine peace which they have learned to recognize and experience.

The Madonna counts on the pilgrims who return to their homes very much. She invites them to be *"instruments of peace"* and *"apostles of love."* The phenomenon of Medjugorje in its worldwide development could not be explained without the drawing force of the testimony of those who have been there. Sometimes there is tiresome and counter-productive fanaticism. There is always someone who experiences even the most beautiful spiritual reality superficially.

The love of truth and the sense of the pastoral are called for, yet especially from the point of view of the pastors, who must consider an event of the reawakening of faith among the most significant of this century. Who has done all this? Perhaps a small community of Franciscan friars with our human limitations? Perhaps six youngsters neither better nor worse than many others who attend our churches?

The event of conversion, especially when it takes on the proportions of a new Pentecost, requires a spiritual sensitivity in the light of divine wisdom.

CHAPTER 7

Nothing is more important than prayer

THE MADONNA IS THE LIVING PRAYER

The messages of Medjugorje, even in their brevity, represent one of the most profound teachings about prayer which have ever been given to Christian people. In them are manifested an absolutely exceptional experience of God which the common man, even those on the road to sanctity, are not able to know. Certain things cannot be said if they are not experienced. When one speaks of divine realities without living them one runs the risk of sounding like cymbals.

Mary in Medjugorje is the master of prayer as in no other previous apparitions. Every message either directly or indirectly contains an invitation to prayer or a lesson about prayer. She is tireless and not afraid of repeating herself. Prayer is what concerns her the most. The people of the parish have laboured hard to understand this and espe-

cially at first when they would ask themselves where the Madonna wanted to go with her always more urgent requests.

Even for me it has been the same experience. Only with time have I begun to understand the absolute supremacy of prayer. We were raised in a Christian environment where in a few decades the spirit of prayer dissolved. Prayer in families has been destroyed by television. In the parish it has yielded its place to activism. The disappearance of the rosary, of Eucharistic adoration and various devotions, the Holy Mass has survived but with effort.

With the fall of prayer, God has become eclipsed. People live immersed in a practical atheism and even if they say they believe, in reality they live as if God did not exist. A world which does not pray is at the edge of catastrophe. With the vanishing of prayer they have also lost faith in the supernatural meaning of life. A church where one prays little is like a garden without water. It is useless to cover our eyes so we don't see: we are in the presence of a spiritual devastation without precedent. This explains why the Almighty has invited her who is the living prayer to this parched, thirsty earth.

Mary has come down for such a long time on this earth to sprinkle it with her prayer. In a world where there is almost no more prayer she has come in person to pray. "Why do the apparitions last so long?" many ask. She has remained for so long to give us her prayer and to teach us how to pray. Her all-consuming desire is that *prayer begin to rule the whole world.* (Oct. 25/89)

Who more than Mary could teach us to pray? Mary is prayer made flesh. All her being is in prayer. She prays ceaselessly in heaven where she presents to God our prayers united by her intercession, but at the same time she descends to earth in a spirit of prayer where she invites us to pray with her.

The visionaries pray during apparition times. They always preserve the concentration of prayer even when they are speaking with the Madonna. In the beginning the Gospa would remain much longer with the visionaries, to illuminate them, to teach them and to comfort them. Now she comes almost exclusively to pray and when the Madonna speaks, she does so to invite us to prayer.

The perseverance of Mary during this long time is impressionable. From the first message she confirms the substance of what will be the basis of her program: *"Dear children! Sympathize with me! Pray, pray, pray!"* (Apr. 19/84) The Madonna wants us to share in her interior life, which is that of continuous prayer. She desires that we have the same principles as she, which are those of a heart which prays incessantly.

However, people do not understand. There is no doubt that the parish has labored to accept the requests of the Madonna who asks for the rosary in the family and Holy Mass every day. The invitations of Mary have asked for everyone, even the old and the children; above all the young people, especially those united in groups, who have answered with more generosity. The Madonna has continually had to encourage and on some occasions to warn not to give any more messages if there was not a response to her invitations.

In many circumstances she gives thanks for the prayers, the fasting and the sacrifices. On several occasions she asks for them with a touching humility like a beggar who is in need. How many times she says: *"Your prayers are necessary for me!"* In some cases she reprimands without means to an end as when she says: *"You pray little"* or *"You are far away from prayer,"* or even more bitterly: *"You are so cold!"*

Nothing about the life of the parish escapes her vigilant gaze. Probably there wasn't a shortage of those who limited themselves to making expert reflections on prayer. We know that especially in our times in which we pray little, there is instead a surplus of scholarly studies about prayer. But the Madonna goes to what is essential: *"I do not desire"* — she says — *"you to speak about prayer but to pray."* (April 25/91)

With the apparitions of Medjugorje heavenly prayer has come down to the earth in the person of Mary. It is all about a call which on the lips of the Queen of Peace has the force of an ultimatum. Has her invitation been listened to? It is difficult to say. After such a long teaching from on high, prayer seems to still be suffering in our hearts, in our families and in our parishes. Is our Church a community of prayer in the heart of Mary? Have the people of God understood that *"nothing is more important than prayer?"* If we would understand it and if we would live it the Madonna would not have come in vain, and for the world a future of light would begin.

LET PRAYER BE LIFE FOR YOU

Studying the messages of Medjugorje offers the most profound and at the same time the most accessible collection of literary passages of teachings on prayer. We are consoled at least in part in thinking that what we haven't understood about the messages of the Queen of Peace could represent the daily spiritual food of future generations.

First of all, we must bring to light that for the Madonna, prayer is the source from which springs forth all Christian life. We often ask ourselves what are the roots from which the Christian draws his vital sap. In our times, for example, we have insisted much on charity as the qualifying characteristic of Christianity. In other times the accent had been put on faith. These are valid perspectives, each of which has its own reasons.

The Madonna in Medjugorje makes prayer the soul of the spiritual life. On various occasions she does not hesitate to affirm that prayer is to be placed in first place and that nothing is more important. In a world where many are inclined to consider prayer to have little effect and to be even useless, the Madonna confirms that it is the thing that is the most necessary and represents the condition of maximum activity of the Christian.

I remember the terrible years of the Bosnian war. What would not have been done to stop it? Who does not remember how much was done on every level to block the tremendous carnage? While many people of good will were acting on the level of charity, diplomacy was moving with uncertain and unsuccessful steps. The blind forces of violence seemed unstoppable. It almost seemed that Satan would succeed in imposing his law of death and the last word would be up to the armies.

I remember during a blockade, a Croatian soldier stopped me and I took advantage of this and asked him how the war was going. He answered that they needed arms. I replied that it was much more important to pray. He answered that in Israel the Muslims pray but it is the Israelis who command with weapons in their hands. But the Madonna thought

War-damaged church in Jarmina, Croatia

much differently about this. Years before she had said that with prayer and fasting wars can be stopped, however violent they are.

The fight between Serbs, Croats and Muslims was only in appearance. At the root of it was a decisive confrontation between the forces of good and the forces of evil. When the war raged, the Madonna indicated who the real actors in the fight were: *"Satan is strong and wants to sweep away my plans of peace and joy and make you think that my Son is not strong in His decisions."* (Aug. 25/91)

No one doubts that in His actions God also uses human agents. Does He not use David to knock down the blasphemous Goliath? David however came out the victor because the Lord was with him. In the final analysis it is the force of God which determines the victory. Even the Madonna has fought her fight, with her small army which she had prepared and it is the one fought with the weapons of prayer, fasting and love of one's neighbor.

At the outbreak of the conflict, Mary clearly indicated what the weapons of victory were to be: *"Dear Children! Today I invite you to pray for peace. At this time peace is being threatened in a special way, and I am seeking from you to renew fasting and prayer in your families. Dear children, I desire you to grasp the seriousness of the situation and that much of what will happen depends on your prayers and you are praying a little bit."* (July 25/91) The people complained because there were not enough weapons with which to fight. Mary instead lamented about not enough prayer, which she considered decisive in determining the course of the future events.

The Madonna teaches that prayer is the decisive weapon in the battle of life. This is valid for the serious circumstances of war, but more generally for whatever situation exists. In fact, in prayer is found the meaning of life, rest in fatigue, decision for conversion, victory in the fight against Satan, the winning of peace in our hearts, the understanding of the will of God in daily events. Prayer allows us to recognize the mission with which God entrusts us, lets us advance on our road to sanctity, lets us find the solution for every difficult situation, helps us to obtain special graces, aids us in helping our brothers, even assisting the souls in purgatory and allows us to co-operate in a effective way with Jesus and Mary for the fulfillment of their plans of salvation.

In prayer, says Mary, *"You are much more beautiful"* but above all we can live, already on this earth the peace and the joy of God which He communicates to those who pray.

From this picture it is clear that for the Madonna, prayer is not one of the duties of the Christian. It is not an activity like the others. It is not a practice or a devotion. It is the fundamental activity of man; it is the truth of his being because man has been created to be oriented towards God and in prayer he manifests his openness to the infinite and his yearning for eternity. *"Prayer"* — observes the Madonna with an all divine wisdom — *"is what the human heart desires."* (Nov. 25/94)

The Queen of Peace has coined a very penetrating expression to indicate the centrality of prayer in the Christian existence. She urges us saying: *"Let prayer be the life of each one of you."* (Aug. 25/89) To live and to pray is the same thing. In reality one cannot live without praying, as a flower cannot live without water. We often ask ourselves why the world in which we live is so populated with death and desperation. The reason is that today the sun of prayer is eclipsed from the heart of many people and their life is reduced to a long and cold winter night. Is there a way out? The Madonna has no doubt about it: *"Pray to be able to discover the greatness and joy of life which God gives you."* (May 25/89)

IN PRAYER YOU WILL FIND GOD

The insistence of the Mother of God on prayer is in perfect symphony with the teachings of Jesus and His apostles. If this seems excessive to us, it's because in our heart the evangelical spirit and the sense of the supernatural have become subdued. Mary understands the true sickness that ails the contemporary world: the increasing abandonment of God, accompanied by the illusion that we can plan the future on our own and with just our power. In the foolishness in men's hearts, there's the thought that they can construct their future independently, without recognizing and accepting their Creator.

There's only one medicine for this insidious spiritual sickness: the return to prayer. In fact, thanks to it man can find the God that he has lost and that he absolutely depends upon. Our Lady knows only too well that in today's world there's much talk about God. Isn't it true that even the secular mass media often discuss the idea of returning to what's 'sacred'? We cannot deny that the topic of religion gets an 'audience.' On television debates, without exception, one of the invited guests is a priest. But Mary's vigilant eyes see a great void: *"Dear children! These years I have been calling you to pray, to live what I am telling you... You talk, but do not live [it]."* (Oct. 25/93)

It's not by talking, but by praying that today the world can rediscover God. Here we enter the heart of the messages of Medjugorje. Mary's intention is to bring back to God a society that has turned its back to Him. From this perspective at the bottom of her message, what is in a certain sense the main part, is her call to conversion. And what is conversion if not the return of man to God? But this can only take place through prayer. To find God one must start to pray.

We will not encounter God by talking, nor in discussions or by studying. God communicates to man through prayer. God is prayer and in the language used by the Queen of Peace they are two words which identify one another. The greatness, the importance and the absolute necessity of prayer are so because in prayer God is present and communicates to man. I had difficulty understanding this truth even though it's simple. Yet, this is what the Church has always taught, defining prayer as "elevating our soul to God." Through prayer Mary wants to lead contemporary man to a live encounter with His Creator.

Our Lady begins by telling us that in our daily living there has to be some time *"consecrated to God."* Consider, however that it is not a time when we are with others. God cannot be put on the same level as other things that preoccupy and fill our daily working lives. *"Putting God first in our families"* is what she often repeats. But how are we to do this? We make prayer the soul of how we live each day. In fact, it's by encountering Our Lord that everything we do takes on meaning and value. So, it's necessary that each of us can say to himself, *"Now it's time to pray. Now nothing else is important to me, now not one person is important to me but God."* (Oct 2, 1986)

Prayer is opening our hearts to God it's, *"the joy of an encounter with the Lord."* (Aug 16, 1986) This is what Our Lady wants us to understand: God is neither unknowable, nor inaccessible or far away. To encounter God and to talk to Him we need not line up like we do when we wait for important people in this world. He shines His grace on everyone, like the sun does on a field of flowers. God is accessible; we can carry Him in our hearts and God is intimately close to us. Our Lady shows a way of prayer that will bring the heart of man to meet the love of His Creator.

Our Lady stresses in her numerous messages the interpersonal aspect of prayer. In a world that has been seduced by the Eastern methods of meditation, including some Christian communities, Our Lady brings us back to the evangelical simplicity of prayer: our relationship of love with God. Prayer is neither for the learned nor the beginner and it doesn't require many techniques. The only thing necessary is a humble and ready heart so it may flower in all its beauty. *"I don't know what else to tell you because I love you and I want you to comprehend my love and God's love through prayer."* (Nov. 15/84)

We begin to truly pray when we experience God. This doesn't happen all at once, but gradually because even prayer life is a long journey. In any case, no one should fool himself into thinking that they have started praying if, at the end of his prayers, he hasn't stayed even for a moment in the presence of God with eyes and heart fixed on Him alone. Prayer is this private one-on-one with God, with Mary, with the angels

and saints. From this intimate relationship bloom all forms of adoration: thanksgiving, praise, petition, the call for forgiveness and love.

When we have the grace to experience God in our prayer, we have already taken the first important step in our journey of faith. When God touches our soul we are never the same again. Man experiences within himself a sweetness and a longing for the Absolute which mark him for life. Many men today live as prisoners of the earthly life and sadly consume their existence like silkworms in a self-constructed cocoon of anxiety. This happens because they have never experienced the Infinite in their hearts and have never wanted to dedicate any space to personal prayer.

It is in prayer that man encounters God, giving significance to his life. The Madonna stresses the important connection between prayer and the meaning of life. Trying to discover the meaning of life distresses many lives, particularly the young. How many persons today feel themselves empty and don't know what to do with their lives? How many debates and how many useless words on the suffering of life torment the most developed and richest part of the world? What is the diagnosis? The Madonna is decisive about this: *"Your life is empty without prayer."* The therapy is precise and significant: *"You will discover the meaning of your life when you discover God in prayer."* (July 25/97)

By embracing God and knowing His love, one receives the light to discover the presence of God in everyday life. It is not true that the world carries on under the blind force of chance and of human impulses. The omnipotence of God bends events to His projects of love. *"Pray, live my messages and then you will see the miracles of God's love in your everyday life."* (March 25/92) It is thanks to prayer that we figure out the signs of the times; we comprehend the plans of God and our place in them for their success. *"In order to understand what you have to do, little children, pray and God will give you what you completely have to do, and where you need to change."* (Feb. 25, 1993)

Prayer then becomes the light which illuminates the road God wants us to travel. In it we discover our mission and find the strength to carry it out. The Madonna repeats many times that it is through prayer that the great choices of our lives are made, *"deciding for God"* and dedicating ourselves to His service. It is thanks to prayer that we become completely His: *"Little children, the more you pray the more you will be mine and of my Son, Jesus."* (June 25, 1994)

CHAPTER 8

Pray with the heart

WE LEARN TO PRAY BY PRAYING

In Medjugorje prayer has returned to the centre of the Christian experience. The persistent teaching of Mary has shaped the parish, and through the pilgrims, has colonized the earth with prayer groups. The natural energy centre is the parish church of St. James but around it different centres of prayer and contemplative communities have formed. In a particular way, prayer has been born again in families where the development of the modern way of living was running the risk of suffocating it. The invitation of the Madonna to *"turn off the television"* at the beginning of Lent in 1986 has remained memorable.

We do not know how the Catholic Church will orient itself in the future in evaluating the events of Medjugorje. Presently, the Holy See has intervened and has taken upon itself the ultimate judgment. However it leaves people free to organize private pilgrimages. The most significant development in Medjugorje is the reawakening of prayer, that is, a return of prayer to the centre of the life of faith for millions of people. The pilgrim who returns from Medjugorje begins to pray like he had never done before.

The Queen of Peace is above all a teacher of prayer. The same invitation to conversion, which is the most important message which the Madonna gives in Medjugorje, is woven into the path of prayer. We are converted by beginning to pray and we advance in changing our hearts by the measure by which prayer conquers and fills it. When the heart is

69

converted, then prayer of joy bursts forth like a fountain of gushing water towards eternal life.

You cannot understand Medjugorje if you don't start to pray. Those who don't pray don't understand it. In a Church where some of the clergy and religious families have put prayer on a secondary plane, the strong and insistent message of the Queen of Peace has fallen onto poorly cultivated soil. The length of time that Mary has been with us indicates how difficult it is to bring the Christians of our day back to the heart of the Church's life, which is prayer. It needs pointing out to some superficial critics that the Madonna in Medjugorje speaks little but prays much. Mary's parish in Medjugorje, with all the limitations and defects which human beings have, is undoubtedly the place in the world where one prays the most and the best.

I am not one of those who love to cite the words pronounced privately by the Pope John Paul II in favour of Medjugorje, even if it would be totally justified. I limit myself to note that the greatest encyclical written by the chosen son of Mary is about prayer. He wrote an encyclical written not with a pen but with the example of life. The Pope of Mary was in the first place a man of intense prayer. It is from this secret and mysterious source which he drew the courage, strength, wisdom and superhuman dedication to fulfill his highest ministry.

After many years of daily apparitions, we can speak of a real and proper teaching of the Queen of Peace regarding prayer. There is no doubt that she has taken the parishioners by the hand and has led them to the heart of the Gospel. It has not been a theoretical but a practical teaching. The Madonna has taught us how to pray by praying. She has reawakened prayer from the depths of the heart through the dedication to begin reciting the simplest prayers of the Christian tradition.

A very interesting fact about this is the testimony of the visionary Marija given at the studios of Radio Maria in Italy: "In the beginning the Madonna had asked us to pray the seven Our Fathers, Hail Marys, Glory Bes and the Creed. It was the first prayer that we learned to recite with the Madonna. We didn't know how to recite the rosary because usually our grandmother led it and we were of that generation that was forgetting. But then we began to pray the Our Father, the Hail Mary and the Glory Be to the Father, sometimes all night until the morning and in this way we began to feel prayer a little at a time."

I have often heard Vicka tell the pilgrims the very precise teachings of the Madonna. Our Lady was above all concerned to teach her *"angels,"* as she first called the six visionaries, to pray and to feel prayer in their hearts. The Madonna does not suggest any complicated meditation techniques, as are in fashion today, even in some Christian settings. Her lessons are always characterized by the simplicity and clarity of the Gospel. She began her doctrine of prayer, inviting the recitation of the Our Father, the Hail Mary and the Glory Be to the Father, and then meditating on  the meaning of every single word and trying to grasp the significance of each word with the heart.

I remember how much St. Theresa of the Child Jesus referred to this. She loved to pause on every word of the Our Father to understand its profound significance with her heart. Many times, however, she would remain fixed on the word, "Father" and contemplating the divine paternity of our relationship, her eyes would fill with tears. This is a very meaningful example of how prayer of the heart begins. It is a matter of feeling the significance of each word pronounced when praying with our hearts.

The visionary Marija, particularly sensitive about the call to prayer, told us of the road travelled to arrive at prayer of the heart. "In the beginning we were praying so that the Madonna would continue to stay with us, then we began to feel the need for prayer and through it the necessity to understand the Madonna more, to stay closer to Jesus, to understand Him more and to feel His presence through prayer. In this way we began to experience our small growths, our small steps, which each of us was travelling, always praying more and more. I remember when, in the prayer group we began the nightly adoration, and around three in the morning we felt sleepy. Then, realizing that that hour was our weak moment, we began to read and to sing the Psalms, and in this way we got to four o'clock. At five o'clock the priest would arrive for the Mass and at six o'clock we would return to our homes. After a night of prayer we were so happy. We were full of joy as we greeted the still sleepy people who had just woken up and were leaving their houses. In this way we began to feel this need and this sweetness of prayer, and that man does not live by bread alone but also by prayer, which has become for us, life."

An experience which many pilgrims have in the first person is described here with valuable existential realism. It is a digging toward the depth of the heart, like searching for a spring of water. In the beginning what we need is to break the external crust, made up of laziness, narrow-mindedness, worldliness, superficiality, and even sins. How many believers pray only with their lips! How hard it is for the prayers of the Scribes and Pharisees to die in man! After the initial effort, which needs perseverance and good will, the Holy Spirit 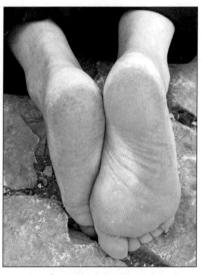 stirs up the desire for God and His grace. In that moment we enter into living prayer, and as the Madonna confirms, *"the joy of meeting with the new-born Jesus."* (Dec. 11/86)

At the beginning the Gospa presented prayer as an assignment to carry out with attentive and serious diligence, but her objective is to lead those who follow her to the experience of joy. After the first steps are taken, prayer can seem like hard work but at the end of the road it is a joy which, once the human heart has tasted it, *"you cannot live."* (Nov. 25/94)

FIRST STEP: TO OPEN THE HEART

The lessons of the Queen of Peace on prayer mirror a road of growth which she has taken with the parish, and through it, the pilgrims coming from every part of the world. This is not a matter of abstract and general suggestion. The Madonna is a concrete teacher and full of educational wisdom. Those who have followed the messages from the beginning have realized that they have been led a spiritual program by means of successive steps. Mary has taken us by the hand, like children unable to walk, and with the passing of time has trained us to climb the challenging but fascinating summit of sanctity.

The essence and centre of the messages of Medjugorje is the heart. It is an expression of the biblical flavor which we encounter very often. We should not be surprised that the 'Daughter of Sion' refers to this expression which reappears again in the Bible more than a thousand times. On the other hand one of her more insistent invitations deals with reading Sacred Scripture in the family. The Madonna wants her messages to be received with the heart and not just out of curiosity. One should fast from the heart from habit. Prayer should come from the heart in total abandonment to her.

What does all this mean? What a great expert of man is Mary, aware of our ingrained tendency for superficiality and the fact that we are ready to listen with one ear and to forget with the other. Like the grain fallen on uncultivated soil, her teaching risks being quickly smothered by thorns and by brambles. From here comes the pressing request to welcome into our hearts and to live all that she teaches us.

Our call through our personal experience is one of the most significant and original aspects of the spiritual journey that begins in

Medjugorje. The Madonna is quite removed from an abstract catechesis. Christianity is not so much a doctrine as a way of life. Mary invites you to understand, to receive and to live. The program which she recommends brings you to experience in your heart the greatness and beauty of life when God is present and enlightens it. In the way we learn to pray by praying, so we understand the faith by living. If we don't live it in our hearts, we cannot feel either God, the Madonna or grace.

For me, this has been one of the features of Medjugorje which has been carved into my life the most. Being used to devour one book after another, I was under the illusion that it is possible to know the faith by studying it. In reality, faith is life and its growth is fruit of an existential journey. Others have understood that they carried a habitual Christianity on them made up of exterior practices and of moral principles, without a living experience of God and of His grace. The Madonna has taught us to live the faith more profoundly and to grow in daily duty.

On the journey toward prayer of the heart, there are three steps that the Queen of Peace mentions in the development of her teaching: the first step is to open the heart; the second is to purify the heart; the third is to surrender the heart to her. Fulfilling these three fundamental steps, prayer's final end pours out like an inexhaustible spring of joy and peace which anticipates the experience of paradise in our hearts.

What does the invitation to *"open your hearts"* mean? When, dear friends, do we open the door to our home? When someone knocks. Hearing the knocking, we decide whether to open or not to open. This is what happens in the spiritual life. Grace passes and knocks at the heart of man. The initiative is always God's who loves us and worries about the eternal salvation of our souls even when we are far from Him and we live in religious indifference or in the mediocrity of apathy.

The grace which has mysteriously taken numerous pilgrims to Medjugorje prompts them to conversion and to change their lives. It is a decisive moment which can mark a person for good or for evil. One can reflect and think about what to do. God places the steps to fulfill and the decisions to make in front of him. Perhaps it could be to give up a mistaken life or a concrete sin. The battle is all in the heart where one can decide whether or not to welcome God's invitation.

The Madonna, who reads all hearts, knows this key moment in the life of a person well and her invitations are multiplied without rest. *"I beseech you, open yourselves and begin to pray."* (March 20/86) *"Open your hearts to God like the spring flowers which crave for the sun."* (Jan. 31/86) *"Pray and change your life."* (Nov. 13/86) Facing our hesitations and the alibis of our unrepentant flesh, she does not hesitate to awaken us with a decisive tone: *"God has given a free will to everyone, and it's in your control."* (Jan. 30/86)

Finally, it is all about *"deciding for God."* This is perhaps the expression which best embodies the persistent invitation to open our hearts. It is a choice that can happen only with the support of grace and which marks the beginning of prayer of the heart. With this brave decision, we take all the sin which weighs on our lives and offer it to the Lord. (Dec. 4/86) He will conquer it in His love, let our lives be reborn and send us on the voyage of holiness and peace.

As much rejoicing there is in heaven for a repentant sinner, so much Mary exalts for the opening of our hearts. *"Today I thank you for every opening of your hearts. Joy overtakes me for every heart that is opened to God...Pray all the prayers for the opening of sinful hearts."* (April 18/86)

SECOND STEP: PURIFY YOUR HEART
The opening of the heart is the first and fundamental step along the road to prayer. Only from a contrite heart can all the graces of prayer for help rise to God: "From the depths I call to you, O Lord; Lord listen to my voice." (Psalm 130) But the pilgrim who returns from

Medjugorje, after the joyous experience of reconciliation with God in the sacrament of penance, finds himself travelling a narrow road full of danger.

The preoccupation for things of this earth returns which distracts us from prayer. (May 9/85) The occasions of sin reappear and Satan, in spite of being pushed away, threatens us with another seven worse spirits; the new condition needs an even greater effort of prayer. It is a question of working from the source to destroy the deep roots of sin from our hearts.

The Mother of God follows the first efforts on the road to purification of heart with a watchful eye, sustaining and encouraging us with images often taken from the daily experience of the parishioners: *"Today I wish to tell you to begin to work in your hearts as you are working in the fields."* (April 25/85) On another occasion she observes with a totally feminine elegance: *"You are finding time for cleaning even the most neglected areas, but you leave your heart aside. Work more and clean with love every part of your heart."* (Oct. 17/85)

Unfortunately it is in this phase that many become tired and return to their previous bad habits. It is enough to recall a real and proper maternal reprimand that the Madonna directed to the parish by means of a long message to Mirjana. *"My dear children, I have come to you to conduct you to purity of soul and therefore toward God. How have you received me? At the beginning without believing, with fear and mistrust toward the youngsters that I chose. Then a majority accepted me in their hearts and began to put into practice my maternal requests. But unfortunately this did not last long. In whatever place I go and my Son is with me, Satan goes there too. You have permitted him to take the upper hand, without knowing it, so that he could dominate you...Do not surrender, my children! Dry the tears from my eyes that I cry watching what you do."* (Jan. 28/87)

The abandonment of prayer, the return to mediocrity, the resumption of old sinful habits are the great risks which await the pilgrims after the first enthusiasm. How to escape unharmed from this temptation which harvests victims with full hands? The Madonna gives only one directive, which is really and truly a maternal cry: *"Return to prayer! Nothing is more important than this,"* she exhorts in the same message to Mirjana.

There are many of those who fell by the wayside after the enthusiasms of the first days. Did not Jesus himself put us on guard to temptation once we have put our hands to the plow? Those who persevere on the narrow road, where the daily toil of virtue is required, are unfortunately relatively few with respect to the multitudes that were called. Nevertheless, if one has persevered on the road to prayer, he will arrive at the moment of grace in which prayer will spring forth like a fountain of joy from the depths of his heart.

THIRD STEP: SURRENDER YOUR HEART

The road to perfection, according to the teachings of the great mystics, foresees three stages, which with a careful analysis can also be seen in the messages of Medjugorje. After the decision for conversion and the fatigue of purification, one enters the third stage which is that of the intimate union of the soul with God. In this phase, as St. John of the Cross explains, the soul is quite passive, in the sense that it trusts itself to the sanctifying work of grace.

The Queen of Peace, after having lead her children to the opening and purification of the heart, wants to bring them to the centre of the spiritual life, which consists in the intimate union with her heart and the heart of Jesus. When it concerns removing the deep roots of sin, our good will is no longer enough. We are so incapable of seeing the sin which is in us and of transforming ourselves into new creatures, that the only thing left for us to do is to offer ourselves to the actions of the Holy Spirit.

In this light, the invitations of the Madonna to give to our hearts to her so that she can change them are understood. When I was listening to this invitation for the first time, I could not understand what she wanted to say. How many times did I ask myself, "What does the Madonna want of us when she asks us for our hearts? What does it mean to give your heart to Mary?" Certainly any one of us can repeat these words and make this offering in prayer, but the real problem is to know how to match our feelings with this.

Then slowly, I understood that there is a phase in our spiritual growth in which it is the Madonna herself who takes the initiative. She asks us for total abandonment to her so that she can transform us in the image of her heart and dress us in her holiness. *Today — she says — I call you to give me your heart so I can change it to be like mine."* (May 15/86) In this concluding phase of prayer of the heart Mary wants to make us participants of her own desires, to offer her prayer on our behalf and to clothe us in her virtues.

When we are united in the heart of Mary, we cannot but live her life which is radically oriented toward God. All the true devotees of Mary love God with the same heart as Mary. Only he who has not experienced the presence of Mary in his life can cultivate the fear that Marian devotion could enter into competition with God. Towards this the Madonna uses stupendous images full of poetry and significance: *"I — she says — call you to surrender to me so that I can keep on presenting you to God, fresh and without sin."* (Aug. 1/85)

Certainly it is an elevated and supreme road on which the Madonna wishes to lead us. Nevertheless, even having to count the extent of our every day fragility, there are many who have begun to taste the sweetness of the prayer which Mary herself gives us when we entrust ourselves faithfully to her. The common Christian sees in the Madonna a mother to whom we can pray. But this is not enough for Mary. She wants us to pray with her and to pray like her, sharing profoundly the beats of love from her heart.

Only then does prayer transform itself, from a daily assignment to accomplish with care, to a joy which is no longer possible to live without. When I hear the Madonna speak of the joy of prayer, I understand that she is talking about her prayer in which she desires our participation in. She wants to tells us about that paradise of which her heart is full: *"Prayer is joy — she repeats many times — prayer is what the human heart desires."* (Nov. 25/94)

Is it a reachable goal? Anyone familiar with the lives of the saints knows well that they have experienced the joy of prayer. It is that joy which is in God and that He gives to us in prayer. The Madonna wants this to be the experience of all the people of God because we are all called to holiness by means of prayer.

We Christians are very often sad and despairing, as those who are without God and without hope in the world. This is because most times we have not experienced the love of God. Christianity has remained a superficial, instead of a living, experience of salvation. How to come out of this painful condition in which too many find ourselves? The Madonna points out a simple way, effective and available to all: *"Renew prayer, until prayer becomes a joy for you."* (Aug. 25/97)

CHAPTER 9

Pray constantly

The Madonna has guided the parish and the pilgrims toward prayer of the heart. She has acted like a mother who helps her children to grow, recognizing their frailties but also their potential. She never tires of repeating the same things, above all for those children who having first put their hands to the plow, turn tiredly around. Whoever has followed the lessons of the Queen of Peace from the beginning has a heart full of gratitude for the infinite patience with which he has felt encouraged and accompanied in prayer. On the other hand, the Madonna herself has affirmed that she has remained with us for such a long time because she desires to teach us to pray.

In comparison with the parish, the Mother of God has proceeded with wise steadiness. First she asked for the recitation of the seven Our Fathers, Hail Marys and Glory Bes which corresponded to a pious tradition of the people of that area. Successively she asked for the daily rosary and one day of fasting during the week (Fridays). Shortly after, the apparitions were moved to the parish church. There, every night, the Holy Mass was celebrated. The Madonna then asked for a second

day of fasting in the week (Wednesdays) and the three mysteries of the rosary each day.

One day on the eve of the Assumption (August 15), while the visionary Ivan was praying in his house and was on the point of coming to the church for the evening liturgy, he had an unexpected apparition and the Madonna told him to tell the people this message: *"I would like the people to pray along with me these days. And to pray as much as possible! And to fast strictly on Wednesdays and Fridays, and every day to pray at least one Rosary: the joyful, sorrowful and glorious mysteries."* (Aug. 14/84) This directive of the Madonna to pray the entire rosary was accepted by the parish, and so the first two rosaries are recited before the evening Mass and the third is recited in thanksgiving after the end of the Mass.

As you can see the Madonna is very practical. She does not limit herself to reminding us to pray but points out the road to travel and the undertaking to assume. We cannot arrive at the incessant prayer of the heart and the experience of joy if we don't make some time each day for prayer. This is so we can commit ourselves to live again in our innermost beings the simple but profound prayers of the Christian tradition.

Before entering actively into the prayers that the Queen of Peace recommends, it seems to me very important to pause and reflect on the amount of time necessary to dedicate to prayer. This is because prayer is one of the themes of her ongoing maternal reminders. How much must we pray? A fundamental question, because man lives in the dimension of time.

In a society where daily life has become a wheel that turns without stopping and where there is no longer any distinction between day and night, between the times for work and those of rest, and where time has become like a rushing river which drags us away, the Madonna helps us to put the day in relationship to God and to include the fleeting moments of our lives in the light of eternity.

Why does most of mankind, especially in the West, spend its life enclosed in the dark space of limited time? They live like ants in an anthill, intent only on running, working and producing. Human existence is chained to the iron cycle of birth, growth, work, labour, sickness and death. There is nothing more tremendous and more desperate than a conception of the world in which the heavens are empty and life has no future. A sign of this perverse wish to eliminate the supernatural are the attempts to cancel the day of the Lord to make it a day like all the others. In this way time is totally desecrated and uprooted from any reference to eternity.

Mary turns to this poor humanity immersed in the shadows and in the darkness of death and invites mankind to come out of its asphyxiating prison. How? By finding time every day for prayer: *"During the day, find yourself a special time when you could pray in peace and humility, and have this meeting with God the creator."* (Nov. 25/88)

Therefore, the first step is to find time in the day for God. Without this decision it is not possible to meet God and let Him enter into our existence. Each day is a measure of our response to the Gospel message. Every day has its own worries, says Jesus. He teaches us to ask our heavenly Father for our daily bread. So that our day is not a shadow which quickly disappears, it is necessary that there be a path toward heaven, from which the light of eternity can filter.

On different occasions the Madonna insists on the necessity that in our daily life there be times in which we are alone, detached from the world, from preoccupations, from the thoughts and worries of life. Then we can be in front of God, in our littleness and humility, to listen to His word, to feel His love and to let us be illuminated and warmed by His light. In the secular passing of time there needs to be this 'sacred' moment. We need to take the firm decision to 'consecrate' some time every day to God: *"Little children, you cannot open yourselves to God if you do not pray. Therefore, from today, decide to consecrate a time in the day only for an encounter with God in silence."* (July 25/89) It cannot be

said that the Madonna was listened to on this decisive point, that is, the road to prayer. In fact she returns there insistently even in the most recent messages, making us aware that without dedicating any time to prayer it is not possible to experience God and His love. *"Open your heart* — she insists — *and give time to God so that He will be your friend."* (June 25/97) *"I desire, dear children that during this time you find a corner for personal prayer."* (July 25/97) From this decision the way to conversion and new life starts on which the sun of the divine presence shines.

Once this fundamental step is accomplished, man meeting God, the desire that the entire day be anchored to eternity becomes always stronger and daily life is oriented toward salvation. How is this possible? The Madonna gives us simple but very effective directions that recapture thousand year-old traditions which were in danger of disappearing especially in families. It is a matter first of all of prayer at the beginning and the end of the day. *"Dear children! God is allowing me along with Himself to bring about this oasis of peace. I wish to call on you to protect it and that the oasis always be unspoiled. There are those who by their carelessness are destroying the peace and the prayer."* (July 3/86)

The day must begin in the name of the Lord and with His blessing. The morning prayers are a task that single people, personally and every family (particularly where there are babies or children), must accomplish with much diligence. The morning is a very important time which can decide the atmosphere of the day. Satan is ready to attack us with the throng of distress, of preoccupations, of nervousness, and anxiety with the intention of occupying our hearts and in this way drag us where he wants.

We need to be ready to push him back with prayer so that peace and faith in God primarily occupy our hearts. Then the entire day, whatever we do will be sanctified by the offering, praise and thanksgiving, whatever we do: *"Pray* — says the Madonna — *that your life be joyful thanksgiving which flows out of your heart like a river of joy."* (Oct. 25/88)

Prayer which illuminates the beginning of the day with the light of God the Creator is also needed to end our day, so that it belongs to Him completely: *"Let your morning begin with morning prayer* — says the Madonna with the concern of a mother who follows us with watchful eyes during the whole day — *and the evening end with thanksgiving."* (July 25/95)

We know how evening prayer, be it personal or with the family, has been destroyed by the television, the internet and by the rhythms of life in which there no longer are distinctions between day and night. Mary teaches us to rest with the Lord, opening our hearts to the action of grace, for the protection that He has given us throughout the day, perhaps without our even being aware of it. We need to thank Him for the immeasurable benefits which He continuously offers us, with the attention of a Father who provides for each of His creatures not only on the spiritual plane but also on the material. (April 25/91)

If we end our day as grateful children of God and with the appeal for pardon and peace, then even when we awake we are more inclined to prayer. Prayer will become a living source which begins to gush from the heart without ever being exhausted. Daily work, because of the labour and the attention it requires that might draw us from God, is transformed into a blessing if illuminated by the light of prayer: *"Dear children* — says the Madonna — *today I want to say to pray before any activity and to finish every work with prayer. If you will do this, God will bless you and your work."* (July 5/84)

In the intentions of the Queen of Peace, prayer becomes a light which illuminates every moment of life with eternity. It is like a fire which needs to be stirred up frequently before it goes out. Prayer is for the soul what daily food is for the body. (Jan. 25/92) It is like the water which the flower needs every day so that it doesn't wither. It is the beat of love of the heart where God lives. No instant must remain without prayer. *"Without unceasing prayer you cannot experience the beauty and greatness of the grace which God is offering you. Therefore, little children, at all times fill your heart with even the smallest prayers."* (Feb. 25/89)

There is no doubt that a set time is necessary to dedicate to prayer. No day can be devoid of morning and evening prayer if we don't want it to dissolve into nothing. But then it is also necessary that every day of our lives is consecrated to God in prayer (Jan. 25/98) with prayers in the morning, evening, before and after work, before and after meals …and finally with the smallest prayers or petitions.

In this way time is ransomed from emptiness and desperation and every instant of life achieves great importance for eternity.

WHERE TO PRAY?

Man lives not only in time but also in space. In the same way that there are times for prayer, there are places for prayer. There is no doubt that when it comes to personal prayer, every place is right. Who is going to prevent us from praying wherever we find ourselves, on the street, in the car or at our work place? In this case the heart itself is the sanctuary where we meet God in prayer. The Madonna even invites us to go to nature to discover God the Creator and to thank Him for all that He does.

Nevertheless, in the messages of the Queen of Peace, there is a reminder that hits us by the force with which it recurs: it is family prayer. Certainly there is just as strong an invitation to attend church either for Holy Mass or for adoration. Repeatedly and ardently, she exhorts us to heartfelt prayer before the cross. But where the Madonna expresses a particular concern is for family prayer which is certainly the most threatened today.

In the past not only were the morning and evening prayers recited in families, but even the holy rosary. During my first trips to Medjugorje it was fairly easy to find homes in which there was fasting and prayer. With the increase in the number of pilgrims, family life, busy with work and disturbed in their normal rhythm, suffered considerably. The presence of groups of people for whom to prepare breakfast, lunch and dinner not only interrupted family prayer but even the regularity of daily Mass.

In this frame of reference, we can understand the seriousness of the Madonna calling the people to family prayer even going as far as warning not to give any more messages. The objective difficulties because of work in the fields and in receiving the pilgrims were not a valid alibi for her. Nothing could justify the absence of family prayer. It was not just about individual prayer at home but also about communal prayer with members of the 'united family.' (Feb.14/85)

What is the reason for so much strictness? The Madonna is profoundly aware that the disintegration of the family is one of the greatest evils of the modern world. To avoid this, she invites us to prayer, in which faith is reinforced, hearts are united and mutual love is nourished. The family that prays preserves itself from the grave wounds which endanger the relationship between couples and between parents and children. In prayer, the family achieves its vocation so well put in the light of the call of the Second Vatican Council to be 'domestic Church.'

The Madonna clearly points out the significance of family prayer. It is the sign that God has been placed in first place and that He lives in our homes with His peace and His love: *"You say that Christmas is a family feast. Therefore, dear children, put God in the first place in your families, so that He may give you peace and may protect you not only from war, but also in peace protect you from every satanic attack."* (Dec. 25/91) We cannot say that God is in first place in our families if prayer is not in the first place!

But what prayer? In particular, the Madonna has at heart the rosary and reading the bible which she desires to place in the framework of the united family: *"I request the families of the parish to pray the family rosary."* (Sept. 27/84) The invitation to read Sacred Scripture instead is something new, especially in the Catholic sphere, where reading of the Word of God happens usually in church during the Mass: *"Dear Children! Today I call on you to read the Bible every day in your homes and let it be in a visible place so as always to encourage you to read it and to pray."* (Oct. 18/84)

It is an invitation which returns many years later, with the requirement that reading is a function of life and of the religious education of children: *"Little children, place the Sacred Scripture in a visible place in your family, and read and live it. Teach your children, because if you are not an example to them, children depart into godlessness."* (Aug. 25/96) It does not just mean a cultured reading, but with wisdom, where the heart seizes the spiritual nutrition of the Word of God and tries to make it his own, by living it.

Has the invitation of the Queen of Peace to read the Bible in the family been accepted? It is difficult to say. It is nevertheless a great novelty for Catholic families of our times, who are not very accustomed to reading the Bible. But it is not this way if we look at tradition, where from the first times of Christianity and through the centuries, the Bible has represented the daily bread with which the faithful were instructed in the faith. It is enough to look at the great cathedrals of the Middle Ages where painting and sculpture offered to uncultured populations the possibility to see and to meditate the story of salvation. The pressing invitations of the Madonna in Medjugorje can nevertheless launch a new era, in which the Bible is the great book of the faith, to which each day the family draws to live and to be a witness.

WHICH PRAYERS?

The teachings of Mary in Medjugorje not only bring us to the discovery of the uplifting greatness and the absolute dominance of prayer but point out concrete times and places and underline the importance of some fundamental forms of prayer. The pilgrim who arrives before the church of the two bell towers finds nothing which sparks his curiosity or his thirst for novelty. This often characterizes the search for the sacred on the part of many people. The prayers to which Mary calls us are traditional prayers which we have partly forgotten or which we partly live.

I am not in the least embarrassed to say that in that oasis of prayer in Herzegovina, I have understood more deeply what I had been taught from my early years on the knees of a mother and that which I had assimilated in long years of study in the seminary. I discovered perhaps for the first time the great value of prayer before the crucifix to which the Madonna called us numerous times, especially during Lent. In my life I have reintroduced moments of daily Eucharistic adoration. In my youth these were called "visits to Jesus" and they are sources of great inspiration, of courage and of renewed energy in confronting the daily obligations especially for those priests involved in apostolic work.

But the two that is most in the heart of Mary is the rosary and the Holy Mass. I have often asked myself why the holy rosary is so dear to the Madonna which, as compared to Lourdes and Fatima, here she requests the complete fifteen mysteries. The Madonna insistently requests this from everyone, in a particular way from the pastors, the priests and the religious men and women so that they can thereby instruct others.

It has struck me very much when, on the occasion of the anniversary of the apparitions, the visionary Marija asked the Madonna if she had a message for the priests. It is quite rare for the visionaries to make these requests of the Madonna who, on many occasions, does not respond. But on that solemn occasion, when numerous priests from every part of the world were present, the Mother of God answered in this way: *"I invite you to call on everyone to pray the Rosary. With the rosary you shall overcome all the adversities which Satan is trying to inflict on the Catholic Church. All you priests, pray the Rosary! Dedicate your time to the Rosary."* (June 25/85)

There is no doubt that, considering the importance of the rosary, Medjugorje recaptures Lourdes and Fatima with even more strength and wealth of inspiration. The daily recitation of the entire rosary, personally and at least in part in the family, constitutes one of the undeniable requests of the Queen of Peace. The rosary is the prayer, par excellence, of she who crushes the head of the serpent and is therefore the most effective weapon to tackle the menacing works of evil:

"Dear children! Today I call you especially now to advance against Satan by means of prayer...Dear children, put on the armor for battle and with the Rosary in your hand defeat him." (Aug. 8/85) A few years later she added another masterstroke to this dramatic and suggestive picture: *"Pray and let the rosary always be in your hand as a sign to Satan that you belong to me."* (Feb. 25/88)

How to justify the extraordinary importance which the Virgin attaches to praying the holy rosary from a theological and spiritual perspective? Undoubtedly it is a matter of a devotion well rooted for centuries in the Church and recommended by the Popes many times. Is this enough? I have often forced myself to enter in the heart of this prayer to understand its greatness. I believe to have found the secret of its value in the biblical texture of the mysteries which nourish the faith, and in its simplicity and humility which make it accessible to all, even to those who are illiterate.

But the most real and profound reason was given by the Madonna herself when she invited people in the church, especially the priests, women and men religious to recite the rosary and to teach it to others: *"The rosary, little children, is especially dear to me. Through the rosary open your heart to me and I am able to help you."* (July 25/97)

In the prayer of the rosary Mary gathers us into her heart; she makes us participants of her prayer, she dresses us in her holiness, and she gives us to Jesus, *"a harmonious flower."* (May 1/86) During the rosary she is in us and we are in her, and if we pray with our hearts, Mary works to change us, to purify us and make us always more like Jesus.

In this light we can understand the reason the rosary precedes and concludes the Holy Mass in Medjugorje. The Queen of Peace asks specifically for the three rosaries every day and also daily participation in the Mass. (Jan. 25/98) It is all about moments which are intimately joined together. Mary prepares and concludes the Eucharist with the holy rosary. Jesus is at the centre. She introduces us into His mystery and arranges us to live it. At the end of the celebration in Medjugorje, the exit stampede of our parishes is missing, and with the recital of the last rosary, we stop with Mary to adore Jesus in our hearts and prepare to live the Mass in our lives.

In various messages the Madonna reminds us of the mystery of the Holy Mass when Jesus comes alive in our midst. She invites us to consciously participate in it and receive Jesus in our purified hearts and make it so that every Eucharist is *"an experience of God."* When we go to Mass *"with joy"* and *"with love"* and we live it *"consciously"* then we can experience all its *"beauty."* We *"receive it"* in our hearts and we *"live"* it in our daily lives.

The picture of prayers which the Queen of Peace calls us would not be complete if we did not make reference to personal prayer, to which we have already referred to when speaking of the prayer of the heart. Unceasing prayer which the Madonna wants to bring us to wouldn't be possible, if our hearts were not the temples in which to adore God in spirit and in truth. *"Children* — says the Madonna in a message — *in the silence of the heart, remain with Jesus, so that He may change and transform you with His love."* (July 25/98)

As St. John of the Cross teaches, we can pray continuously in whatever we are doing, if we have "a loving attention" to the sweet presence of Jesus. The lips and the mind are quiet and in this supernatural silence, prayer reaches its climax. In the abandonment of faith we offer Him ourselves and our poor lives, and He changes and transforms us with His love. And by means of this highest form of prayer, we can always be with Jesus to continuously taste of His divine friendship.

CHAPTER 10

I beg you, be converted

YOU HAVE TAKEN THE ROAD TO RUIN

In Medjugorje I learned the essential things, those which count, and the real criteria with which to interpret life and the society in which we live. The world judges itself with its own variables which are, however, very different from those of God. Immersed in the world, we Christians are profoundly influenced. We even run the risk of being the blind pretending to guide other blind, with the final prospective of all falling together into the same pit. (Matt 23,16)

Today humanity is at the mercy of a great moral confusion. In those countries with ancient Christian roots, immorality spreads even to provoking astonishment in representatives of other religions. The Muslims, Hindus and Buddhists accuse western society of spreading atheistic materialism and moral corruption in the world. They are right in large part. Where the Gospel and Christian holiness had once blossomed, we now support the return of paganism, the erosion of virtue and the exaltation of evil.

Many believers are swept away by this new mentality which abolishes sin and proclaims everything licit and allows everything, even that which is contrary to the law of God. The voices, like that of St. John the Baptist, raised to say to modern man: "It is not permitted!" (Mark 6, 18) are rarer and weaker. The heroic effort of this accusation often weighs heavily on the shoulders of the Holy Father, while too many Christians are silent and conniving with evil.

The Madonna in Medjugorje, at least in her public messages, does not indulge in apocalyptic descriptions regarding the imminent future, neither does she indulge in that pessimism without hope which characterizes many self-styled private revelations. She does not divide the world into the good and the bad, into the pure and impure and into the saved and the lost, according to the language of the sects. She stoops maternally over a world which has chosen the road to ruin, away from God and at the mercy of sin, and calls it back to the road of salvation with a strong and passionate voice.

The diagnosis which the Queen of Peace makes of contemporary society has traces of raw realism which leaves us breathless. She sees things from God's point of view, who values not the material or technical progress but the moral and spiritual situation of mankind. The judgment, even if maternally sweetened by the grace of the Madonna, doesn't leave any space for nuance. It is necessary to look at the gravity of the sickness in the face so we can accept the suffering and work for the cure with courage.

The gaze of Mary on the world goes beyond appearances. The Madonna certainly doesn't allow herself to be deceived by the glitter of fleeting things. She observes the heart of man and sees that it is far from God. Already on the second day of the apparitions, real tears fell from her eyes because man was not at peace with God. But her heart cries *"tears of blood because of the souls who are lost in sin."* (May 4/84)

Today, some who are hard of hearts and slow to believe, disarm the faithful in the spiritual battle, insisting that hell is empty. Instead, the Mother of God is anguished in seeing her children committing sin, placing themselves into the hands of Satan. Evil is like a tidal wave which floods the world. To the parishioners who complain because she asks for too many prayers, the Madonna answers: *"Dear children! I still need your prayers. You wonder why all these prayers? Look around you, dear children, and you will see how greatly sin has dominated the world."* (Sept. 13/84)

In truth, at some moments we also are aware of it, but then we shrug our shoulders and continue as usual, without reflecting on the road to ruin and death. The Madonna, who is always sweet even when she reprimands, does not hesitate to use hard language when the salvation of our souls is at stake. Her tone sometimes re-echoes that of the prophets and of Jesus when they condemned the destructive force of evil.

On the feast day of the Annunciation in 1992, one of the great occasions when the Queen of Peace appears dressed in golden vestments, the people were waiting for a message of consolation, having been severely tested by the war in Croatia. God knows how much the Mother would have wanted to give it to her children in the vortex of a great tribulation. Instead, one of the most severe and unforgettable messages arrived: *"Dear Children...I have come to you to help you and, therefore, I invite you to change your life because you have taken a path of misery, a path of ruin. When I told you: convert, pray, fast, be recon-*

ciled, you took these messages superficially. You started to live them and then you stopped, because it was difficult for you. No, dear children, when something is good, you have to persevere in the good and not think: God does not see me, He is not listening, He is not helping. And so you have gone away from God and from me because of your miserable interest. I wanted to create of you an oasis of peace, love and goodness. God wanted you, with your love and with His help, to do miracles and, thus, give an example. Therefore, here is what I say to you: Satan is playing with you and with your souls and I cannot help you because you are far away from my heart. (March 25/92)

When I listened to this message, I tried to console myself as much as possible with the thought that perhaps the Madonna was referring only to Bosnia-Herzegovina, where the war raged and with it the hate, with those terrible manifestations which filled public opinion with horror. But in reality the eye of Mary embraces all of humanity which is *"unfaithful and walks in darkness,"* a humanity which wants to develop its future without God and for which therefore, *"there is no future or joy and, above all, there is no eternal salvation."* (April 25/97)

It is clear that the Madonna presents a scenario painted in dark colours, which nevertheless we are all able to verify by looking around us. We are facing the hightide of evil. Mary's goal however, is not to push us towards a despondency without a solution but to provoke the reawaken-

Fr. Svetozar Kraljevic at destroyed Franciscan church in Mostar during civil war.

ing and the counter-attack of the forces of good so they prevail over evil. She has come just for this, "to sustain us in the moment of trial" and to transform the times in which the prince of this world dominates, into times of grace and benediction.

It is very important therefore to understand that we are living in the moment of the great seduction — the extreme attempt of Satan to take humanity away from God. Only in the awareness of the great battle to which we are called can we encourage Mary's plans for the return of the world to God.

In the years of the civil war in Bosnia-Herzegovina, the people lived moments of dangerous moral confusion. Even among the people of Medjugorje, the poisonous ideology of ethnic separation was slithering around like a snake. Some were openly saying that the Croatians, Serbs and Muslims had to be exiled to their own areas, without taking into account that for years, if not for centuries, the three groups had lived together side by side. This perverse diabolical suggestion became a sign of the loss of morality by a humanity seduced by Satan.

The Madonna multiplies the reproaches, almost foreshadowing the strategy of evil to drag the entire world into the spiral of the great seduction: *"Dear children — she cautions — I invite you all to prayer and renunciation. For now as never before Satan wants to show the world his shameful face by which he wants to seduce as many people as possible onto the way of death and sin."* (Sept. 25/91) It must be said that there is a connection between the times of Mary and those of Satan. When the prince of this world launches the great offensive he finds the 'Woman Clothed with the Sun' (Rev. 12) blocking the way.

Satan exploits the most diverse situations to seduce man. They go from the hate which produces divisions and civil wars to the greed for material goods. His objective however is always the same: to take possession of souls. This, nothing else, is the prize at stake: *"Dear children — Mary affirms — today again I would like to say to you that I am with you also in these troubled days during which Satan wishes to destroy all that my Son Jesus and I are building. He desires especially to destroy your souls. He wants to take you away as far as possible from the Christian life and from the commandments that the Church calls you to live. Satan wishes to destroy everything that is holy in you and around you."* (Sept. 25/92)

These are burning affirmations like a fire in a historic moment, when there is silence about evil, and from certain parts its existence is

93

even denied. Mary's gaze sees where our poor tired eyes cannot reach, because we are deprived of the supernatural vision. She sees the virulence of the devil which with his power *"desires especially to destroy your souls."* (Oct. 25/92)

The Madonna has come to oppose evil in its design to bring the world to eternal ruin. Her will is total and decisive. It is not enough to save just a few souls. She wants to save them all: *"I call you, dear children, to now grasp the importance of my coming and the seriousness of the situation. I want to save all souls and present them to God."* (Sept. 25/91) From this determined will to save us and lead us to the way that brings us to heaven is born the distressed appeal to conversion.

I DESIRE TO LEAD YOU TO THE WAY OF SALVATION

In Fatima the Madonna prophesied the immense spiritual confusion of humanity. Having passed through the great tribulation of two world wars and almost half a century of a cold war, mankind has always surrendered to the diabolical seduction of building a world with only human forces, where man is god. At the beginning of the 21st century, when the great offensive of the diabolical dragon began, the Woman Clothed with the Sun has herself come down into the battlefield. Now that the beast tries to seduce all the earth to bring it to destruction, the Mother of the Church and of humanity intervenes to show us the way to peace, joy and salvation.

At the centre of the great battle is the human heart with its capacity to decide. *"Satan* – cautions the Madonna – *wants to lead you the wrong way, but he cannot if you do not permit him."* (July 25/93) Not even the Mother of God can force our liberty. On various occasions she reminds us that she doesn't desire to compel any one to accept the messages. To her it is urgent that they are accepted with the heart, that is, in freedom and with love.

In her humility she bows to our liberty, but at the same time she reminds us that God had gifted us with a free will which constitutes the greatness and the dignity of the human person. *"I am with you* — she says — *but I cannot take away your freedom."* (Aug. 7/86) Therefore it is all about using free will for good. The Madonna confirms that she cannot help us if we don't want it. Her invitation directs all humanity to an eternal source, where each of us chooses our eternal destiny before God.

This profound respect of Mary for what each of us is, has always impressed me greatly. She has a consideration for us that we don't have

for ourselves. She is perfectly aware that God has created us free and in this rests our permanent dignity as persons. She turns to our hearts to propose, never to impose. She doesn't even use the subtle influences of which we humans are masters when it comes to persuading others.

Mary limits herself to demonstrating the consequences of good and evil and invites us to verify them in our own life experiences. Is it not true that evil hurts us, making us restless and unhappy and leaving us at the mercy of our passions? The Madonna shows us what we do not see in our obstinacy and that is, with evil we place ourselves into the hands of Satan who then leads us to the road of ruin and death. The Madonna has clearly said that hell, where men are eternally lost, is the consequence of human freedom working unrepentantly against God. Is it not true then that goodness frees us and completes us, giving us happiness and even joy, notwithstanding the struggle and sacrifice required?

In her wise teaching, the Queen of Peace clearly points out the road to salvation and the road to ruin and invites us to reflect before it is too late. The appeal to conversion is placed before this dramatic use of human liberty as we face good and evil. The Madonna herself specifies that among her many messages, conversion is the most important. Since the beginning of her apparitions she has invited us to conversion with the same insistence as that of prayer. There is an intimate connection between the two messages. If we pray it means that the road to conversion has begun and is going forward.

The conversion of heart is a grace that she asks God insistently on our behalf but at the same time it is our response to the gift of grace.

(April 25/98) The Madonna invites us to decide for God but she herself cannot choose for us. From here come the dramatic appeals which are born from the heart of a mother who does not resign herself to seeing her children become prey of he who wants to destroy and lose them for eternity. *"[I] implore: Convert"* is her cry of agony. (March 25/97) And also: *"Choose the life and not the death of the soul."* (March 25/96)

Here we are at the heart of the messages themselves of the Queen of Peace, where their profound evangelical inspiration emerges. Did not the preaching of Jesus begin with the same appeal? "Repent and believe in the gospel," (Mark 1:15) were the first words of the preaching of the Divine Master. As He had come to save, so Mary has come for such a long time to show us the path to salvation which consists of the world returning to God: *"God gives me this time as a gift to you, so that I may instruct and lead you on the path of salvation."* (Aug. 25/97)

Has this sorrowful but so essential and decisive appeal been accepted for the eternal destiny of each one of us? This is the real question that concerns Medjugorje. All the other discussions including the ones regarding the ecclesiastic approval of the apparitions do not seem to have a great importance for the Madonna. Our return to God is her only interest. If this happens, all the rest will be given to us as bonus. But what sense does the official recognition of the apparitions make if they have not reached their purpose, which is the eternal salvation of this generation without God and without peace?

Have we listened to the continual invitation of Mary to change our lives and to return to God? First of all, each of us must examine himself and then perhaps we can look around us. It doesn't seem that the Madonna is at all content with our response, and she lets us catch a glimpse in one of her recent messages: *"Little children, I wish to make of you a most beautiful bouquet prepared for eternity but you do not accept the way of conversion, the way of salvation that I am offering you through these apparitions."* (July 25/95)

However there are signs of a new life even if they appear like rare flowers. When I go to Medjugorje I always see long lines in front of the confessionals and every day I meet someone who has begun a new life in that blessed place. We are perhaps far from that springtime that the Queen of Peace ardently desires, but these gems which sprout here and there on trees stripped by winter ice leave the heart open to hope.

GIVE ALL YOUR PAST TO THE LORD

How is one converted? Whoever has lived the experience of conversion knows that it is first of all a grace. The man in sin is as if dead and if the breath of the Holy Spirit which gives life does not empower him, he will never be able to recover on his own. The first touch of grace provokes the reawakening of conscience which saves us from a life imprisoned by sin. The divine light shows us our miserable and desperate condition. Like a slowly forming stream of water, from our still hardened heart, the longing for goodness and regret for our lost innocence begins.

We look at ourselves and see, maybe for the first time, the devastation that sin has done to us, destroying the goodness and beauty of our soul. We thought that we were free and happy and instead we find ourselves in slavery and degradation. We have no more respect for ourselves and are intolerable in our own eyes, finally able to see our miserable condition. The evil one has us chained by our passions and is ready to assault us with all the terrible means available, in case we should think about escaping.

You understand that we have chosen the road of death and that the only valid decision to take is to turn back. But we hesitate. A whirlwind of thoughts assault us. How will we manage to change our lives? How will we be able to live without those things which we have greedily fed ourselves with until now? What will people think and how will our friends, to which we are tied, react? Satan gives us no rest. He doubles the seduction, trying to convince us that we will never be able to live without what he has to offer. He suggests that the path to which God is calling us is absurd and impossible.

What is needed is the sweating of blood for conversion. The forces of hell unfold all their powers of seduction and terror. Mary and the saints pray for us. The outcome of the great battle which decides the eternal destiny of our soul depends on us. Whoever has gone through a moment like this knows that we are at the fork of the road which marks our life. The result is uncertain. We are tempted to let it go, to resign ourselves to remaining on the path of death. Satan convinces us, without our knowledge, with subtle arguments. He whispers in our ears that God is not here, that death ends it all and that the hereafter doesn't exist. Then why not enjoy our life?

Understand, however, with that almost perceptible light which is still in you, that on this road you will fall into the abyss of eternal perdition, while the horror of the kingdom of evil provokes dismay and fear. It is the moment of prayer. It is about your very first prayer since you crashed headlong into the abyss where grace has come to visit you. If your cry for help rises to God, if you invoke mercy and pardon for yourself, you begin the most important of all your endeavours, that of conversion and salvation.

How many people have lived this drama in their pilgrimage to Medjugorje? Countless, each in a unique way, but profound, authentic and decisive, as the confessors well know. Here they have waited hours and hours for the lost lambs to fall on their knees before them, to ask for God's forgiveness on their wayward lives and for absolution of all their sins.

These are the great wonders that the Queen of Peace performs in Medjugorje. These are the real resurrections from the dead. The millions of pilgrims who have been in this place of grace have testified that they have been touched by God. This reawakens faith and gives rise to the desire for a new life.

The Madonna is the great director of these changes of heart, the mother of conversion and the refuge of sinners. It is Mary who invites us to place our lost lives into the great arms of Divine Mercy and to begin a new life with courage. *"Dear children! Today I want to wrap you all in my mantle and lead you all along the way of conversion. Dear children, I beseech you, surrender to the Lord your entire past, all the evil that has accumulated in your hearts. I want each one of you to be happy, but in sin nobody can be happy."* (Feb. 25/87)

Yes, God gives us the possibility to be reborn and to begin a new life, without counting our mistakes, however serious they were. God gives people the possibility to start everything from the beginning and to become saints even if they have touched the bottom of degradation. If we give Him our sin in the sacrament of confession, He destroys it in His love.

The Madonna certainly looks with pleasure at the numerous priests that are available for confession in Medjugorje, as opposed to many other Christian parishes. She herself invites the faithful to the confessional because only with the sacrament of reconciliation, and not by our own judgment, can they be certain of being in the truth and in peace: *"You cannot, little children, realize peace if you are not at peace with Jesus. Therefore, I invite you to confession so Jesus may be your truth and peace."* (Jan. 25/95)

In confession the Immaculate Heart of Mary triumphs. In the decision for God new people are born who inaugurate new times. Many times Mary reminds us that we are living in a *"time of great grace."* First of all, it is the grace of conversion that God pours on *"a world of sin."* And it is through *"personal conversion"* and not through who knows what terrifying events, that a new world will be born on which will blossom the civilization of love.

The great turning-point in the story of humanity, which the Mother of God has come to ask for, passes through the heart of each of us. As there has been a personal refusal of God and of His Holy Law, in the same way there must be a personal decision for God and union of each heart to His Holy Will. Initially there is a commitment to yourself to change *"your own life"* and to *"change all the negative in you, so that it all turns into the positive and life."* (May 25/91) Only then, after having brought our own conversion to completion, can we help others to be converted.

The Madonna knows our hearts deeply. She knows that initially the good wheat grows, but then the thorns of daily preoccupations risk suffocating it. Countless are her reminders to follow the path to conversion in daily life, trying to change each day, through the practice of the virtues and living the love of God and neighbor in all His nuances. Conversion along which she guides us is a daily journey which never ends *"like insecure children in their first steps,"* (Dec. 25/89) until we have arrived at *"a full conversion."* (June 25/90) Then joy will overflow from our hearts.

Never in any preceding era has humanity touched the abyss of evil and sin as it has in our time. We are the living the greatest moral confusion that the story of the world has ever known. But the Divine Mercy has wanted that the most pressing summons to conversion would echo right now so that where there is an abundance of sin, there is an overabundance of grace.

CHAPTER 11

I desire to lead you all to complete holiness

SANCTITY IS THE PURPOSE OF LIFE

Extreme sickness calls for extreme remedies. In a world where sin dominates, the Queen of Peace lets the invitation to conversion and holiness resonate. Perhaps the appeal to conversion is more comprehensible to a majority of people. Calls for holiness results in more uncertainty, as if the commitment to become saints should be reserved for some particular categories or states of life.

I remember that the first invitations to place ourselves on the road of holiness were made by the Madonna in 1985. I was going to Medjugorje for almost a year and in the prayer groups they were passionately discussing about Mary's call to become saints. Some remained almost fearful, because in traditional mentality, sanctity corresponded to a particular charism and not to the Christian way of living, which could also be very simple and humble, even if pure and without sin.

That invitation of Mary, repeated with maternal insistence in the succeeding years, manifested itself by entering many hearts, and more than any other thing helped people to understand and put into practice that universal vocation to sanctity which forms one of the highest ideals of the Second Vatican Council.

In the messages of Medjugorje, a very clear and linear vision of human existence is manifested. Mary is a great gift of God the Creator, whose beauty and greatness we are called to discover. Nevertheless, instead of the way to salvation, man often chooses the path of ruin and death. This is true above all in our times in which sin is abundant and it seems that the evil one reigns. Driven by love, God invites the Madonna to reawaken faith in order to rouse us from sin and direct us on the way to salvation which brings us to heaven.

Even from the beginning the Madonna has never ceased to invite us to conversion. She does so even in the most recent messages and with such a sorrowful heart that it makes us think the world is still

distant from a response that gives God joy. However, at a certain point in her long stay among us, she has begun to invite us to holiness, not some group in particular, but all of us without distinction.

This universality of the summons is confirmed from the first message in which the Madonna points out the objective of sanctity: *"Dear children, if you live the messages, you are living the seed of holiness. I, as the Mother, wish to call you all to holiness so that you can bestow it on others."* (Oct. 10/85) Putting aside doubts about her intentions, the Madonna emphasizes that her messages are for *"everyone"* and they are holy and complete, (May 25/87) using the lives of the saints as examples. (Sept. 25/94)

The vision of human existence to which the Madonna wants to open our hearts is defined by means of these reminders. We are dealing with leaving a life of sin and beginning a new way, the way to salvation. It consists of letting the fruits of grace be born in us, through an evangelical existence crowned by the splendor and beauty of the virtues, whose coronation is love and whose fruit is joy, real joy, which the world does not know and cannot give.

"Now, purified of your sins, I want to guide you ahead in love," (Dec. 26/85) says the Madonna to the parishioners almost wanting to display her program for a spiritual life. After the moment of conversion, the road of salvation knows the stages of purification and the labour of virtue. Then comes the climb into the last phase of the walk of sanctity, which is the stability in grace in the fire of love and union with God.

The Madonna suffers for all those who have started the walk but then have looked back and remained in their previous life of mediocrity and sin. At the same time, however, she doesn't hesitate to take those of good will by the hand with the offer of bringing them to the sublime peaks of perfection. In the messages of the Queen of Peace, the ways to sanctity coincide with the way to salvation. Our own sanctification is the unforsakeable goal of life, where once reached, we can attain the endless joy of eternity.

Sanctity is the heart of the Christian vocation. Every follower of Christ has to begin his life as a walk of perfection. The Mother of God returns to these themes innumerable times, well aware that they require a new mentality from which we are still very distant. She is not content to point out the saints as examples but she proposes even the martyrs as a model of life who would die testifying: *"I am a Christian and love God over everything."* (Nov. 25/97)

Mary in Medjugorje invites all the faithful who in large part are simple, humble people, to a perfect sanctity which does not need to fear anything, not even martyrdom. Some could even think that the Madonna exaggerates. In reality she tries to revive in the hearts of believers the essentials of the Gospel. Is the Christian life not an imitation of Christ? Has the Divine Master not asked us to follow Him on the way of the cross to Calvary where He himself has achieved martyrdom? Certainly to our mediocre, soft-soled Christianity, words like sanctity and martyrdom seem exaggerations. Mary reminds us that they are essential parts of the Christian existence in which we must allow the life of Jesus Christ to relive in us.

Certainly the Madonna has taken on a great assignment, inviting us on the walk of holiness. She knows our weaknesses and our afterthoughts. She knows that Satan easily seduces us with material things and *"misunderstandings, the non-understanding and non-acceptance of one another."* (Jan. 25/90) Mundane things are enough to cause us to surrender to discouragement and to the calls of the world. She knows this and therefore she has remained such a long time with us, that she *"might teach [us]*— she says — *how to make progress on the way of holiness."* (Jan. 1/87)

It is a question of a life which no one can deny. In fact it is through this path that we can obtain peace and joy. We realize the purpose of earthly life in the light of eternal salvation. The Mother desires that her children be like her. Mary is Full of Grace and All Holy. She is the fully realized human being. In the Virgin the infinite sanctity of Jesus Christ is reflected as in no other creature. Should we be amazed that she sets us on the road that she has taken, so that we too can clothe ourselves with the splendor of her beauty and fill ourselves with the fullness of her love?

I have never noted any symptoms of fanaticism in Medjugorje. The faith of the people is the same as that of good Christians in our parishes. You can note the same traces of simplicity on the faces of the people who come on pilgrimage. I have never seen excesses of any kind, not even in prayers, which like uninterrupted music, flows humbly and joyfully in the hearts of many people. The manifestations of religiosity preserve the sober rank of the peasant culture, made up of actions more than words. And yet in that environment of daily simplicity, you notice the invisible yet present perfume of sanctity.

It is certainly not the kind of holiness to which we are accustomed, as if we must be people with exceptional charisms to follow it. Mary in Medjugorje teaches us to navigate the road less traveled, made up of prayer and sacrifices, of faithfulness to daily duties and acceptance of the cross. She wants sanctity in family relationships by means of forgiveness and mutual acceptance. The model which she proposes is that of her own sanctity which flows humbly and silently across the streams of daily life. No one however, can reject this finish line which is the end of life itself.

SANCTITY IS A WALK WITH MARY

After the joy of conversion, the labour of virtue begins. They are the first two stages on the road to eternal salvation. The messages of

Medjugorje call those who are far away to conversion and urge the undecided and the lukewarm to holiness. Mary sows with her hands full, but how many are the grains which grow to form the mature ear of the wheat of Christian perfection? The Madonna knows well that her invitations to the road of holiness are often not even understood.

It is clear that we can't decide for such a challenging project if we don't at least notice its value and significance for our lives. The first thing to do is to pray to the Holy Spirit so that He can enlighten our hearts with a ray of His light to awaken in us the desire to live a holy life. If we remain fascinated by His splendor, we can't even find the strength for the great enterprise: *"Pray — she encourages — that you may be open to everything that God does through you that in your life you may be enabled to give thanks to God and to rejoice over everything that He does through each individual."* (Jan. 25/89)

If you have the grace to understand that your life is fulfilled in following and in imitating Christ, you will succeed in resisting the return of sin after the initial enthusiasm and joy of conversion. Satan knows us too well. He waited forty days when Jesus was hungry after which he approached Him with his tremendous force of seduction. He will do the same with you. After you have confessed and have decided to change your life, after you have returned to your daily habits, he waits for the fervour of your prayers to be subdued and the primeval desires to reawaken in you. He studies your weak sides in depth and assaults you with the sirens of seduction and the storm of temptation.

How many give up on the road to holiness at the first difficulty? Certainly, the decision for conversion often needs heroic efforts but God sustains it with special gifts of fervour and joy. Perseverance in goodness and in the practice of virtue by means of daily fidelity in ordinary life is certainly much more difficult. The willingness and enthusiasm to continue may easily be extinguished by dryness and darkness of the spirit. I have known more than a few people who, after a period of eagerness upon returning from Medjugorje, went back to being stuck again in the mud of mediocrity and sin.

The Madonna knows the weaknesses of her children and she comes to meet our frailty, giving us the certainty that on the long, slow and difficult path of holiness, she accompanies us, holding our hand. This is without doubt one of the most radiant and comforting aspects of the messages of Medjugorje. Mary advances with each of us, co-operating with us and sustaining us in the most difficult moments. We do not continue alone on the path to salvation and perfection, but are accompanied, sustained, comforted and protected by her whom God has given us as a Mother. *"My heart* — she assures us — *carefully follows your progress."* (Dec. 25/86) One of the most profound aspects of the maternity of Mary is shown in this way. She is our Mother because she shapes us and helps us to grow, accompanying us until the full maturity of Christian perfection.

One of the most indicative messages concerning this, even if less quoted, was given on the Feast of the Annunciation (March 25). It has always struck me very much for its extraordinary depth even if expressed in very simple words: *"As I bore Jesus in my womb, so also, dear children, do I wish to bear you into holiness."* (March 25/90) Here Mary wants us to understand that we become saints with her, for her, and in her, in the way St. Louis de Montfort loves to remind us. Already St. Augustine had observed that in the way that Christ the head, was created in Mary through the work of the Holy Spirit, so it is necessary that even the members are generated and grown in Mary's womb through the grace of the same Holy Spirit.

We remain fascinated in seeing how the Madonna does not cease reminding us that on the path to sanctity we are not alone, because she is there to guide and instruct us: *"I desire* — she confirms many times — *to teach you and help you to walk the way of holiness."* (June 25/91) On the other hand, she attributes everything to the grace of the Holy Spirit, whom she is used to imploring, praying with her outstretched hands on the pilgrims who are present at the apparitions. She asks us to allow her to transform us: *"May your heart* — she urges — *be prepared to listen to, and live, everything which the Holy Spirit has in His plan for each of you. Little children, allow the Holy Spirit to lead you on the way of truth and salvation towards eternal life."* (May 25/98)

Here we are quite distant from that representation of Christian holiness which is the work of the personal efforts of exceptional men. Unfortunately, this arrangement is difficult to change. We turn to the saints to obtain graces, but we don't absolutely think that God places before us the same road they have traveled. Mary reminds us that the vocation for sanctity is universal and that she herself takes us by the hand like little children who still take uncertain steps to accomplish it. Nevertheless, she states, *"I don't want to compel you to be saints by force."* (Oct. 9/86)

The idea that it is the Madonna herself who takes an interest in the work of our own personal sanctification lifts us and gives us courage. There is the risk that the ideal of perfection, placed before our misery and weakness, may discourages us. Saint Therese of Lisieux consoled herself by saying that she, being too small to confront the peaks of perfection like the great saints, would have to be carried in the arms of Jesus. Mary in Medjugorje encourages us in turn with the most evocative images of her maternal tenderness. She says that she holds us by the hand, protects us under her veil, carries us in her womb, holds us in her heart and is maternally vigilant over every step we take.

One of the greatest graces that our generation has received is the incomparable and sweetest maternal guide of Mary on the road to holiness. There is no doubt this is the assignment the Madonna has received from God until the end of the world. There is no holiness in the Church which is not the work of the Mother of God and the Holy Spirit. No other preceding generation has ever had the grace of such an explicit and public teaching authority to help it proceed with certainty on the road toward eternal life. If we have not brought it to fruition, cautions the Queen of Peace, we will regret this great gift when she is no longer among us.

Sometimes I ask myself if this long and patient reminder of the Madonna to become saints has succeeded in penetrating the hearts of people. I am aware that it is a pretty idle question because each one of us should first of all ask himself if he is dedicating himself to this path.

In this regard, the Madonna reprimands and encourages at the same time, with the wise teaching skill of a mother. *"Already for years you are invited to holiness but you are still far away,"* she reproaches even in the day of the Annunciation (March 25/89). Almost ten years after the first call to become saints, it seems that the situation is still at the beginning stage: *"Now I invite you in a special way, little children —* she says as if she was doing it for the first time *— to decide to go along on the way to holiness."* (April 25/94)

There is no doubt that many have turned a deaf ear and after having put the hand to the plough, turned resignedly around. Sometimes I ask myself how God can put up with us. Evidently He must love us very much for He acts like those mothers who are always ready to excuse their children no matter what mischief they have done. Yet it is enough that someone in the family does well and works for the others to gladden the heart of the Madonna. On the occasion of the great feast of the anniversary of the apparitions, she surprises everyone with an unusual but very encouraging ending of the message: *"Little children —* she says *— thank you for having responded to my call and for having decided to walk with me toward holiness."* (June 25/96)

TOWARD HOLINESS ON THE WAY OF LOVE

The Madonna in Medjugorje invites all of us, without exception, to a perfect life and she gives us the encouraging certainty that she is there to help us. *"I am with you"* is without doubt one of the most recurrent signs of tenderness in her celestial messages. But this is not all. Mary points out even the means by which to travel along the path of our sanctification. There are many reasons for amazement and for meditation, because the Queen of Peace shows everyone a very concrete road, accessible even to the most weak, but whose end is the highest that we can imagine.

Sometimes we think that St. Therese of the Child Jesus was the first to perceive and to show the people of God the little way toward perfection. In reality, the Saint of Lisieux did nothing but recapture the childhood spirit of the Gospel. Under the guidance of Mary, St. Therese lived years of intense and fervent love in her very short life. There is no doubt that there exists a holiness typically Marian, as St. Louis de Montfort intensely perceived, when he described the perfect image of Mary as "the model of God."

What is that type of sanctity which with respect to all the others has a particular Marian flavor? It is the same sanctity as Mary lived during her life here on earth. It is the way of faith and abandonment, of dedication and obedience, of silence and prayer, of humility and love. Mary has not taken centre stage in history. Her existence passed without miracles, in complete obscurity, completing the will of God through the fabric of ordinary life.

This model of sanctity that we could call Marian, showed itself to me when the messages of the Madonna invited us to daily prayer, to small sacrifices, to faithfulness to duties, to small conquests over ourselves, to mortification of our egoistic tendencies and to the search for the will of God through even the smallest things of ordinary life.

At the beginning it seemed that I had returned to my childhood when my aunt, a religious sister, urged me onto this road, telling me about the examples of St. Dominic Savio and St. Luigi Gonzaga. Then I understood better that humility is that soil on which the tree of sanctity grows. That spirit of childhood, of trust and abandonment, is fundamental so that Mary can succeed in guiding and forming us according to the image of Jesus she desires to be reflected in all of us.

Mary's sublime teaching skill has touched me so much. She makes the way to sanctity so simple and easy for everyone that I wanted to dedicate a song of the Magnificat — Mary's poem, to this theme. This composition was born in my heart right in Medjugorje on Christmas 1995. In song number 26, "The Sanctity of Mary," I represented an idea that came to light in my soul in these years. Mary forms us into her particular type of sanctity. The saints, who entrusted themselves especially to her guidance, are distinguished by their stirring similarity with the Mother. In them there is much smallness, humility, simplicity and childlike spirit, as if Mary was taking delight in keeping them little in her arms.

For what purpose does Mary ask for prayer, fasting, small sacrifices, and self denial from those who walk along this road? The objective is the same as the highest point of perfection: to learn to love. Sanctity consists of a heart capable of giving love. It is evidently not about a human love, but a divine love, of which the Immaculate Heart of Mary is full and which she desires to empty into our hearts.

The appeals to return to love like those regarding prayer and conversion are countless. The Madonna is very concrete and from the beginning she encourages us to practice love in the family: *"First of all, begin to love your own family, everyone in the parish, and then you'll be able to love and accept all who are coming over here."* (Dec. 13/84) We

108

are all more available to love those persons who we don't know compared to loving those who are near to us and whose limits and defects we support with effort. But the wise teaching of the Virgin puts us on guard to these illusions: *"Love first of all your own household members, and then you will be able to accept and love all who are coming."* (June 6/85)

In the first years of the apparitions, the policing apparatus of the state demonstrated its intolerant and brutal face. Even among the inhabitants of the village, there were some who were actively collaborating with the authorities to repress a phenomenon which was getting out of hand. When the pastor, Father Jozo, was put in prison, the atmosphere, which was already aggravated by small daily persecutions, risked becoming dangerously inflamed.

The Madonna who also listened maternally to the venting of the visionaries, then still youngsters, was very firm in encouraging them to live the Gospel message. She invited her *"angels"* to greet the police politely when they met them and to the parishioners she would say: *"I am calling you to the love of neighbor and love toward the one from whom evil comes to you…Pray and love, dear children! By love you are able to do even that which you think is impossible."* (Nov. 7/85)

Mary was preparing hearts for the tremendous moment of the war, when the Satanic hate of ethnic intolerance threatened to destroy the seeds of love so abundantly spread out. It was an atrocious experience. The Madonna begged: *"Dear children, pray that from your heart would flow a fountain of love to every person both to the one who hates you and to the one who despises you."* (Nov. 25/91)

After the war the great problem was and still remains that of reconciliation. Mary knows that peace guaranteed by arms has no future if hearts are not disarmed. Here again, she points out the way for real peace.

It is all about a message that can be the base of that civilization of love that we and the Madonna wait for with impatience, as a gift for the third millennium: *"Dear Children! Today I invite you to decide for peace. Pray that God give you the true peace. Live peace in your hearts and you will understand, dear children, that peace is the gift of God. Dear children, without love you cannot live peace. The fruit of peace is love and the fruit of love is forgiveness. I am with you and I invite all of you, little children, that before all else forgive in the family and then you will be able to forgive others."* (Jan. 25/96)

The civilization of love is born in our hearts. It cannot be a political, social or economic project. It is necessary that people learn to accept, welcome and respect each other and to help and forgive each other. The starting point is the family. If you don't love who is near to you, how will you be able to love those you don't know? The new world will be formed by good people, who know how to see in others the face of a brother.

A heart capable of loving his neighbour is what the Madonna wants to mould in us. To show us how dear to her are all the ways of showing love, she invites us to live "The Hymn to Charity" of Saint Paul. (1 Corinthians 13) It is the first and only time that the Queen of Peace expressly cited a biblical passage in her messages, but the fact that she pointed out just this text is very significant for understanding what kind of sanctity she wants from us; *"Glorify God with a hymn of love so that God's love may be able to grow in you day by day to its fullness."* (June 25/88)

The simple walk toward sanctity to which Mary leads appears clearly before our eyes. With prayer, denials, small sacrifices and victory over ourselves, we can open our hearts to the love of God so we can give it to the brothers whom we meet on the road of daily life. Welcoming, forgiveness, smiling; the outstretched hand becomes signs of a concrete sanctity which changes the world and makes our lives serene and even joyful.

How radically different the world would be if we all had a contest to share the love which God pours into our hearts! It would be the beginning of paradise. The Madonna in Medjugorje dares to suggest this extraordinary utopia. To a world torn to pieces by wars, hate, resentment and the segregation that does not even consider the bonds of affection, the Queen of Peace comes to bring the only medicine which can save it: the love of God.

If man would accept conversion and the way to holiness following the path of love, they would not need to wait for paradise to be happy, but already now they could experience paradise in their hearts. Inaccessible project? Impossible for man but not for God. The important thing is that you personally decide to place yourself on the road to sanctity. In the beginning it will seem a difficult and painful road. However, if you begin to travel on it, God will reveal all its sweetness so that you will eagerly take part in every step along the road that brings us to heaven.

CHAPTER 12

Heaven is the goal for which you must aim

YOUR LIFE PASSES LIKE A LITTLE SPRING FLOWER

To Sister Lucia of Fatima's question, where do you come from, the Madonna at Fatima replied that she came from *"heaven."* The reference to the hereafter is one of the defining aspects of the message which comes from Medjugorje. Here the Virgin has not limited herself to showing the visionaries heaven, hell and purgatory, but she brought some of them to the hereafter with their own bodies, which is a very rare experience in Christian mysticism. This fact confers to the apparitions of Medjugorje a unique characteristic among all that have occurred on the earth.

We will not understand the importance and the urgency to the call of eternity if we don't reflect on the situation of the modern world. Here an atheistic and materialistic world view of life is being declared on a grand scale.

Today men think little of eternity. Even a certain number of Christians who go to Sunday Mass nourish serious doubts about life after death. Lately many, being unable to deny the evidence of hell in the Gospels, suggest that it would be empty there. Besides all this, we are struck very negatively by the striking silence which characterizes a large part of preaching and catechesis, on the topic of life after death.

Therefore, we should not be surprised that on such a decisive point of Christian doctrine, which touches on the eternal future of souls, the Madonna in Medjugorje had to intervene in person, in a much broader way than Fatima, to remind us about those evangelical truths which concern our eternal destiny.

We live in a time characterized by an eclipse of God in the heart of man, as has never been seen in the history of humanity. A way of considering life, according to which man comes from matter and is fulfilled in it, has been established. "With death all is finished" said the old sacristan in the celebrated novel "Diary of a Country Priest" by Bernanos.

In the past, this vision of life, which links man to animals, was the idea originating from small circles of libertine and pleasure-loving intellectuals. Today it is inculcated in the classroom, where children are taught about their close ancestry with the chimpanzee.

Death continues to frighten but is banished and hidden. Many men live and get old without knowing where they come from or where they are going. Immersed in the mechanism of materialism, people are born, grow, work, battle, cry, suffer, eat, drink, enjoy themselves, become ill and exit the scene. They do this without any expected future and in general indifference, as if man were a handful of dust. What is there left to do with this vision of life but just chew on whatever bone is offered by the world, knowing that in the end, it is all useless because everything in life comes to an end.

"Carpe diem," (seize the day which is passing), counseled the Latin poet Horace. But is this enough to justify the fatigue of living? Then isn't it also true that without God even the beautiful things of creation end up being piercing thorns and fatal poisons? The miserable condition of man today, walled in the prison of perfection and of sin, often reappears in the reflections of the Queen of Peace in Medjugorje. Here she reminds us of an existence which is more conformed to our dignity of having been created in the image and likeness of God.

On many occasions the Madonna repeats that our destiny is heaven. We are only passing here on earth. We come from God, who created each of us with a purpose for our lives: *"You — says the Madonna in a famous message — are not able to comprehend how great your role is in God's design."* (Jan. 25/87) Each one's life is a realization of the plan of God the Creator. He calls everyone onto the difficult road which is also full of beauty, joy and holiness and which will bring us to the glory of eternity.

The Madonna sees us immersed in a cycle of meaninglessness, of following unimportant material things and objectives, forgetting the eternal destiny which awaits us. On some occasions the Queen of Peace told the parishioners that God wanted to test them using their properties. This happened when inclement weather ruined the crops. It was a question of divine teaching which desires to detach our hearts from false riches so we can begin to appreciate the real ones.

Our life, explains the Madonna, must be viewed by the light of what is eternal. Life is like a shadow which quickly disperses. We do not have a stable residence here on earth. It corresponds to the Christian

view of life, as a pilgrimage from earthly time to eternity. This is what the Mother of God wants to suggest to our hearts. She doesn't do it with those images dear to a certain traditional preaching where the drama of death was painted in dark colours. The Madonna has a delicacy and an incomparable grace in expressing herself, but when necessary, she doesn't hesitate to place before us the hopeless horror of the fires of hell.

She often compares our existence to the flowers of spring, which are splendid for their freshness and the beauty of their colours, but which quickly end. *"Little children* — she says with touching tenderness — *don't forget that your life is fleeting like a spring flower which today is wondrously beautiful but tomorrow has vanished."* (March 25/88) The Madonna never uses any word that despises human life in any way. Instead, many times she invites us in prayer to understand all its value and greatness. But heaven help us if we take possession of it and abuse it on the road of sin. Then it would become a miserable journey toward ruin and death.

What is left at the end of life? How do we want to be at the moment of death? When we have bet everything on things that pass: riches, pleasures, honours, and all the world offers to turn us away from God, what state shall we find ourselves in at the moment of death? What will we bring to the hereafter? We all reach that moment, when it's no longer possible to turn back, because the time we have at our disposal is finished.

The Madonna invites us to wisdom, urging us to choose for God in life, *"Children, decide seriously for God, because everything else passes away. Only God doesn't pass away."* (May 25/89)

From Medjugorje comes one of the strongest appeals to eternity in all human history, to a humanity which grows wicked and drowns in the infernal mud of an atheistic and materialistic idea of existence.

I DESIRE TO TAKE YOU ALL WITH ME TO HEAVEN

In the messages given to the six seers, and in a particular way to the visionary Marija, the Madonna speaks above all about paradise. It is very interesting that she uses both the word "sky" and the word "paradise," both being expressions found in the Gospels. As we will see further on, after death our souls are quickly sent either to paradise, purgatory or hell. Nevertheless, the design of God the Creator is to bring us all to paradise. This is His will and this is the desire of the Madonna. The fact that we can go to purgatory for a time of purification or that a soul can be eternally lost in hell depends on whether we live a grace-filled life or reject it.

The power of this plan which captures the essence of the divine plan for salvation and demonstrates great faithfulness to biblical texts, has struck me deeply. In fact, God has created us for eternal happiness in paradise. This is the project of His infinite love. To bring this to reality He sent His Son and poured out the grace of the Holy Spirit on us. The Madonna co-operates with God so that all can be saved and can be with her in heaven, in the ocean of boundless Trinitarian love.

Life is planned as a walk toward paradise. This is the only road which conforms to the will of God and along which we look toward the happiness which awaits us. The way to ruin and death which brings us to hell is the decision to refuse the love God offers us. Purgatory, even though a state of salvation, is the result of our imperfect conformity to the love of God, who has prepared a place in heaven after the pilgrimage of this life.

The reminders with which the Queen of Peace invites us to go along the way of sanctity, by which we reach eternity, are among the most beautiful that have ever come from a private revelation. The Madonna talks with such a tone of voice that we understand she comes from above. When she appears in her splendour and beauty, more precious than any other description, she brings heaven to earth

To tell us about heaven the Madonna uses a very sensitive expression that everyone can understand: *"In heaven — she says — is the joy."* (May 25/91) What does the human heart desire if not to be happy? In a certain sense joy is the end goal of life because God is infinite happiness, being an ocean of infinite love. The aim of the Madonna on our pilgrimage of holiness and salvation is to bring us to this place of light where she lives with God.

It is remarkable that the most beautiful messages on this theme are given on liturgical anniversaries of saints and the dead. They are occasions in which the Madonna asks us to pray for the souls in purgatory, who in turn will help us to understand that things of the earth are not important and that only heaven is the destination for which we must aim.

Referring to the feast of All Saints, the Madonna touches one of the most sensitive chords of her heart: *"I desire — she says to us — that each one of you who has been to this fountain of grace will come to Paradise with the special gift which you shall give me, and that is holiness. Therefore, dear children, pray and daily change your life in order to become fully holy."* (Nov. 13/86)

The Madonna is our mother and she wants us with her in heaven directly after our death, clothed in her sanctity. It is such a strong desire that it is difficult to restrain. She repeats it again on more occasions: *"I love you dear children with a special love* — she announces in a stupendous message given in the month of November — *and I desire to bring you all to Heaven unto God. I want you to realize that this life lasts briefly compared to the one in Heaven. Therefore, dear children, decide again today for God. Only that way will I be able to show how much you are dear to me and how much I desire all to be saved and to be with me in Heaven."* (Nov. 27/86)

After having reminded us that on earth we are like the short-lived flowers of spring, Mary taking up the same image, with a sublime poetic touch, asserts that she wants to make of us *"a most beautiful bouquet prepared for eternity."* (July 25/95) As it is noted, the bouquet is the arrangement of flowers for the bride. The Madonna is the Queen dressed in gold of Ofir (Psalm 45) who enters the king's room into the heart of God, bringing his sons like a marvelous bouquet of flowers as an offering to the Holy Trinity.

The ultimate reason of her lingering visit here on earth is confirmed by unforgettable expressions: *"You know, little children, that I am with you and I desire to lead you along the same path to heaven, which is beautiful for those who discover it in prayer."* (Aug. 25/90) *"I love you and desire to take you with me to paradise. God sends me to help you and lead you to Paradise which is your goal."* (Sept. 29/94) *"I do not desire for your life to be in sadness but that it be realized in joy for eternity, according to the Gospel."* (Dec. 25/96)

Finally, perhaps the most beautiful passage: *"I am here, dear children, to help you and to lead you to heaven, and in heaven is the joy through which you can already live heaven now."* (May 25/91) The Madonna does not hesitate to insist that by the road on which she guides us, we can already attain happiness on earth, even if there are times of testing, of suffering or of combat: *"I want to lead you all —* she says *— to perfect holiness. I want each one of you to be happy here on earth and to be with me in Heaven. That is, dear children, the purpose of my coming here and it's my desire."* (May 25/87)

THE VOYAGE OF THE BODY INTO THE HEREAFTER

In the catechesis of the Queen of Peace, human life is presented as a walk toward eternity. The appeal to conversion and the invitation to embark on the road of sanctity lead us to heaven where there is joy without end. In no other apparition has the Mother of God outlined the plan for redemption and the meaning of human life with such extravagant clarity. The constant referring to eternity is essential to Christian faith and without it Christianity would be radically falsified.

The Madonna resumes the evangelical message in her inclusiveness, strongly confirming to our generation that only one thing is necessary: the eternal salvation of our souls. "What does it profit a man to gain the whole world — Jesus asks himself — if he then loses his soul? Or what will man give in exchange for his soul?" (Matthew 16, 26)

Nevertheless, today's skepticism about what awaits us after death is so great, and the catechesis about these subjects is so evasive, that the Madonna has performed a deed that has never happened in any preceding mystical experiences. She has taken two of the visionaries and brought them with their bodies into the hereafter to visit heaven, purgatory and hell with her. To my knowledge, a phenomenon of this kind is unique in the entire narrative of the Christian faith. Undervaluing it would be a sign of superficiality.

Whoever, like me, has listened many times through the years to the two seers, Vicka and Jakov, talk about this experience knows that it is a testimony of tremendous seriousness, which we would uselessly try to diminish, or even worse, to disqualify with an unbelieving smile.

Already from November of the first year of the apparitions, the Madonna had shown heaven, purgatory and hell to some of the six visionaries (Vicka, Marija and Jakov). It is interesting to note that in Medjugorje we are presented with the complete state of souls in the

Marija Pavlovic-Lunetti during an apparition in 2004.

hereafter whereas in Fatima, the Madonna had shown the three children only hell.

In addition, differently from Fatima, the Madonna has not been content to show the hereafter in its reality of joy, pain and horror merely in a vision during the apparition. A few weeks after the vision, she took Vicka and Jakov physically in person to see heaven, hell and purgatory. After this visit the two youngsters found themselves here on earth and exactly in Jakov's house from where the Madonna had taken them. She was holding them by the hand, since they were somewhat awestruck, but well aware of what they had seen and heard. Even Ivan confirmed having been transported to paradise in his body. His testimony is absolutely credible but not as unquestionable and solid as that of two persons (Vicka and Jakov) who have been there together.

It is not my purpose to describe the hereafter here in all its particulars as the young protagonists of this incredible experience refer to it. We know that God, in order to teach us, adapts Himself to our way of thinking and understanding. It seems important for me to harvest the essentials, which corresponds exactly to what the Church teaches in this regard.

Paradise is a space of infinite light and of indescribable happiness. Vicka and Jakov noticed that persons are perfect even in their exterior features. In this way the Madonna wanted us to understand that one day souls will be reunited with their bodies again, with the perfection of the risen Christ. Showing the blessed in heaven, the Madonna has said: *"Look how full of happiness the people who find themselves here are."*

117

Purgatory is a place of suffering. Vicka and Jakov state that they did not see any people but only a dense fog inside of which could be heard shouting and crying. Regarding the souls who find themselves in purgatory, the Madonna urged us to pray for them so they can go to paradise as soon as possible.

Hell appeared to them as an immense space with a great fire at its centre. When asked, Vicka does not hide the fact that she wouldn't have been able to resist the terrifying spectacle and the feeling of horror and fear had the Madonna not been near her. The two youngsters affirm that they saw people with the features of horrible and unknown animals falling into the fire. The Madonna said that from it is not possible to ever get out of hell and people find themselves there who on earth rebelled against God and His will. Having followed Satan in this life, they will follow him in death

Is this extraordinary testimony believable? The first observation to make is that the youngsters describe the reality of heaven, hell and purgatory with absolute theological precision. The language, images and symbols typical of popular tradition must not let us lose sight of the core of the message. Paradise is presented as a condition of full and defined joy in God; purgatory as a condition of temporary purification which can be shortened by our prayers; hell as a condition of everlasting punishment where the demons and the unrepentant souls burn in the fire of rebellion and inextinguishable hate.

I want to add that it is not easy to give a testimony of this kind before people. Is it not true that today even in churches there is little talk of the hereafter? Perhaps there is a lack of faith; certainly there is a lack of courage. There are not many in the Church who talk about hell as Jesus and the apostles talked about it. The youngsters of Medjugorje don't ever evade the duty of testimony.

I have heard Vicka hundreds of times during the course of many years retelling her experience before pilgrims coming from every part of the earth. She does it always with precision, firmness and loyalty. She has no fear of the smiles of incredulity or sympathy. She fulfils a task that the Madonna entrusted to her. It has struck me greatly with how much certainty Jakov gave his account of the voyage to the hereafter on the occasion of a great meeting at the Palasport of Milan in the presence of almost 15,000 people. There were people beside him, interpreting for him. His testimony coincided perfectly with that of Vicka. He was equally faithful to the messages received and their fulfillment. The Madonna has wanted, by means of these young people, to summon the Church to the urgency of preaching on the ultimate realities which await human life.

THE DRAMA OF LIBERTY

Meditating on the eschatological message of Medjugorje, I have been able as much as it concerns me, to see a little more clearly into the tremendous mystery of eternal damnation. Our hearts become frightened and full of alarm facing it. We often ask ourselves how can God, who is infinite love and infinite mercy, let His creatures formed in His image and redeemed by His blood, fall into the frightening horror of eternal damnation?

The Madonna in her messages explains that God has created us for paradise and tries everything to save us. How many times does the Queen of Peace invite us to meditate on the sufferings of the crucified Christ caused by our sins? The love of God falls on us without limits. Mary's prolonged visit is allowed by God so that all will be saved and be with her in heaven.

Then why does hell exist? To understand something of this mystery it is necessary to take human liberty into sober consideration. The theme of free will and free decisions are among some of the most recurring of the messages of Medjugorje. The Madonna invites us innumerable times to decide for God and for holiness. Even when it comes to the attainment of paradise, a firm decision is necessary: *"My dear children! Today I want to call all of you to decide for Paradise. The way is difficult for those who have not decided for God."* (Oct. 25/87)

Nevertheless man can also not reply and has the possibility of refusing the love that God offers him. Hell is the drama of divine love

offered and refused. It is created by the human decision to separate from God which is life, beauty, truth and love. The consequence is the condition of death, of horror, of lies and of destructive hate which is created in the heart of man separated from God.

Can we perhaps scold the Creator because He doesn't deprive us of our liberty? The Madonna affirms that she doesn't want us to become saints by force and that she can't deprive us of our liberty. Generally her messages begin with an invitation and end with a thanking for having responded to the call. Therefore, the relationship of the creature to the Creator has to be that of love.

But the gift of love, in order to be thus, must be free. The decision for paradise would have no value if a refusal was not also possible. *"God — cautions the Queen of Peace — gives Himself to you, but He wants you to answer in your own freedom to his invitation."* (Nov. 25/88)

Someone could object that the most incomprehensible aspect of hell is its eternity. Why then does God not limit it in its time? The ultimate reason is again to be sought in the liberty of the creature who finds himself in a state of damnation. The demons and the damned who find themselves in hell do not want to convert and submit to their Creator and Lord.

All of this makes us reflect on the greatness of human freedom and on the consequences of its exercise from which depend our eternal destiny: *"God — the Madonna reminds us — has given to all a freedom which I lovingly respect and humbly submit to."* (Nov. 25/87)

Before closing this terribly serious but fascinating theme about the hereafter, I would like to indicate a point of reflection which merits being explored in depth. The Madonna in a justly famous message affirms that she wants to accomplish in Medjugorje what she began through the secrets in Fatima. But the secrets of Fatima included the vision of hell and the devotion to the Immaculate Heart of Mary to save souls which were at risk of falling into it with sin.

In Medjugorje the scenario on the hereafter is enlarged to include the vision of purgatory and heaven. What else could these insights of Fatima mean if not the maternal project of Mary to save the children of this century from the darkness of the abyss and bring them with her to the joy-without-end of heaven? Nevertheless, this grandiose project of the love of God through the maternal heart of Mary flows through our decision to convert and to persevere on the road of sanctity until paradise.

CHAPTER 13

Satan searches for you and wants you

"SATAN IS STRONG"

One of the most vivid experiences that I have had in Medjugorje is the participation in the prayer group of the visionary Ivan. It consists altogether of about twenty people that all these years have been accompanied by the Madonna in a particular way. Ivan is the leader of this group to which for many years even Marija and at times Vicka have also participated. I remember that when Ivan was in the army, the Madonna had asked Marija to lead the group, urging her to accomplish this assignment with seriousness. Marija was struck by that advice.

Generally this group gathers two evenings a week to sing and to recite the rosary, usually on the hill of Podbrdo. Through Ivan, the Madonna guides these young people, by now adults, in a special way, giving them directions for life and asking them for prayers and sacrifices for special intentions. Most of the time, the meetings of the prayer group are exclusive even if some group members, now married, bring their children. On some occasions, however, when the Madonna allows it, even pilgrims can participate in them, and then these have the joy of being present at the apparitions.

I have often asked myself why the Virgin has chosen a particular group of people for herself, more or less the same ages as the visionaries, even though she cares about the whole parish and the pilgrims who arrive there from every part of the world. The group lives like the rest of us in the dimension of faith because only the visionaries see the Madonna. There is no doubt that by means of these people she wants to build a special resource of prayer and testimony. The group preserves all the messages received in these years and through their study, it will be possible to better understand the presence of the Queen of Peace in Medjugorje.

It was on the occasion of a meeting of this prayer group that the Madonna gave a message about Satan that has made a profound impression on me. It was September 1986, on a muggy summer evening. We were crouched one against the other in the thousands on the slopes of Podbrdo. I was struck by the message which Ivan communicated to us after the apparition: *"Satan — the Madonna said — is searching for you and wants you."* A shudder of fear traveled along my back and I understood in a flash of light the profound significance of the biblical images of the roaring lion and the dragon ready to devour our souls. *"He needs only a small crack in order to worm his way in,"* she then added, recalling the image of the serpent ready to exploit any opening to penetrate into our life and there to sow poison.

In that year the Madonna had placed us on the lookout for Satan at least ten times. Altogether there are more than fifty messages in which the Queen of Peace names the infernal serpent. She calls him by name: Satan. She names only him without mentioning the other demons, almost suggesting a battle without borders between her and the prince of evil.

Painting by Aldona Karosas.

A little at a time the true reality in which human life is placed was defined before my eyes. On the one side, object of the infinite kindness of God who wants to lead it to the joy of heaven, and on the other side, a menacing evil that leaves nothing untried in order to take man with him into hell's eternal punishment.

The blanket of silence about Satan is among the most incomprehensible facts of contemporary Christianity. This is not a question of something minor but an essential aspect to the Christian faith. In fact, we cannot understand the value of redemption brought about by Christ if we don't put into the correct light he who opposes Christ with unquenchable pride and hate.

Today's man has lost the sense of evil and its negative force on life. At the same time, he is not aware of the seductive and vicious attacks which permeate the work of the evil one, who because of hate toward God wants to bring man to ruin. Hell, in the thoughts of some theologians, has been reduced to a mere hypothesis; as if Satan was very busy but with no results.

This climate is very favourable for the devil who can thereby act without being disturbed since people are unprepared for the spiritual battle. Who, in fact, would provide surveillance of a house when from every angle they are quick to say there are no thieves? The Madonna in Medjugorje not only places the activities of Satan in their true light but allows us to see how he tirelessly operates with incredible ferocity and trickery. She also reveals his dangerous threats through the traumas of daily life and, at the same time, shows us the weapons with which to fight and defeat him.

"Satan is strong" is the warning that the Queen of Peace gives us many times. However, he is not invincible. The important thing is to be aware of his presence and to uncover his subtle deceptions so we can fight and defeat him with prayer, self denial and love. What are at stake in this battle between heaven and earth are our souls. But while Mary wants to bring souls with her to paradise, Satan wants to destroy them in the inextinguishable fire of hell.

SATAN HAS POSSESSION OF PART OF MY PROJECT

In the messages of Medjugorje there is no abstract teaching about the devil but instead a bringing to light of his perilous concrete activities. In the many years of the apparitions, Satan has been present from the beginning to obstruct the plans of the Mother of God with all his forces. *"Whatever place I go* — the Madonna says in a message to Mirjana — *and my Son is with me, there also is Satan."* (Jan. 28/87)

In every chapter of human history, until the end of the world, the duel takes place unceasingly between the Woman Clothed with the Sun and the Red Dragon of which the Apocalypse [Rev. 12] speaks. On the one hand it is possible to state that Satan makes every effort to become master of Mary's every project of love and peace, but on the other hand we can also highlight the contrary, that the Mother of God victoriously opposes evil in its plans of destruction and death.

When I arrived in Medjugorje for the first time in 1985, I was profoundly impressed by the long series of messages in which the Madonna placed the parishioners on guard against the deceitful activities of evil which was trying to take over her plans. What it was all about remains God's secret. Who can, if not He, see what happens in the depths of our hearts, where with our choices we become sons of light or sons of darkness?

On first impressions, the external situation was better than the actual situation. In spite of the influx of pilgrims, the villages around the parish had preserved an atmosphere of simplicity and seriousness of which today many lament. There was prayer and fasting in families, certainly more than now. I remember the evenings passed in groups tying tobacco leaves onto long ropes, all sitting in a circle, the pilgrims and people of the area, while we sang and prayed. The Medjugorje of the first years has remained in our hearts like the corner of a small Nazareth, now definitely lost.

The Madonna has never shown any preoccupation for the contrary position of the bishop of Mostar or the clumsy and awkward attempts of the state police at the start of the apparitions to intimidate the visionaries and their families, at least on the personal level. Danger was not coming from them. Therefore, where was the cunning serpent at work? Only the eyes of Mary can see him, certainly not ours. Nevertheless, we will have the satisfaction of verifying her suppositions, if we are allowed, when we get to heaven.

It must concern something very subtle which only the expert counterfeiter can plot. The Madonna sounds the alarm even if she does not reveal what side we must guard in order to recognize the danger. First she warns that Satan *"wants to frustrate [her] plans."* (July 12/84) She incessantly reminds us in successive messages of the gravity of the danger, until a year later the chilly announcement:

"Satan has taken part of the plan and wants to possess it. Pray that he does not succeed." (Aug 1/85)

This pronouncement of the Madonna has always struck me. According to Mary, Satan is not satisfied with obstructing or destroying her plans but wants to take possession of them, making them his own and taking her place. How? I have long meditated on this activity of the infernal fraudster. How has this developed in subsequent years? With supreme shrewdness he has succeeded in influencing many Medjugorje groups scattered throughout the world. He has caused them to split up and then to disband. Is it perhaps not true that some of the most prestigious magazines which were born on the waves of Medjugorje then passed on to hosting messages and visionaries of dubious origin, some of which, like Vassulla Ryden, were condemned by the Church authorities?

What can we think of the Madonna's statement in the summer of 1985, that Satan had taken part of her project with the vicious resolve of making it his own project? Evidently it would be rash to suppose, but it seems that the very grave danger that Medjugorje went through didn't consist of external persecutions or in a lessening of the parish's spiritual fervour. In fact the Madonna had confirmed that she was happy about its spiritual renewal. (Jan. 24/85) Perhaps the danger came from the unexpected, the superlative ability of the eternal liar to dress like an angel of light.

I arrived in Medjugorje a few days after the Madonna had directed attention to the great danger. The youngsters of Ivan's prayer group with which I had come in contact, thanks to Marija and Vicka, were particularly busy offering prayers and sacrifices for the victory of the Madonna. The fact that they didn't make any suppositions struck me very much. Evidently the Madonna had limited herself, as usual, only to asking for collaboration without giving way to useless and morbid curiosity.

It was then that I saw how even the smallest sacrifices are appreciated by the Madonna. Once I saw the visionary Marija choosing the most attractive of the chocolates in a box while she said, "This time I don't make a sacrifice and will choose the most beautiful one." Evidently even the choice of a very small chocolate was a sacrifice pleasing to the Madonna who does not despise anything, but values everything, including what appears insignificant.

The message of the first week in September was received with jubilation in our hearts, especially on the part of the young people. After a month of intense prayer and sacrifice, the Madonna said on that blessed day: *"Dear children! Today I thank you for all the prayers. Keep on praying all the more so that Satan will be far away from this place. Dear children, Satan's plan has failed. Pray for fulfillment of what God plans in this parish. I especially thank the young people for the sacrifices they have offered up."* (Sept. 5/85) What had happened? We'll never know for sure, but we know what weapons the Gospa used to win the battle.

SATAN LIES IN AMBUSH AGAINST EACH OF US

This intense and very particular experience was certainly very instructive for whoever lived it up close, participating intimately in the concerns of the Madonna. On the one side, the highly deceitful activity of the evil one and his skill as liar is revealed to us; on the other side, the power of prayer and sacrifices with which the Mother of God will crush his head, has been made obvious.

Nevertheless, during the many years in which the Queen of Peace has stayed with us, her references to the activities of evil are so numerous and concrete that they constitute a precious and irreplaceable fountain of teachings. The Madonna points out the traps which Satan lays as snares in our daily life, the mastery with which he seduces us on the road of evil, the weeds that he sows with an open hand to divide hearts and families, and finally his ultimate objective, which is becoming the owner of our souls, to bring them to eternal ruin.

In reality Mary doesn't say anything new that isn't contained in Sacred Scripture and in spiritual tradition. Our generation however, has lost the supernatural gaze of faith and has misplaced the vision of the real dimensions of the spiritual combat. This dramatic battle involves earth, heaven and hell on whose outcome our eternal destiny depends.

Notable is a message of August 1985 which at first moment left us somewhat stunned when the Madonna admonished the parishioners with these words: *"Dear children! I am calling you to prayer! Especially since Satan wishes to take advantage of the yield of your vineyards. Pray that Satan does not succeed in his plan."* (Aug 29/85) What was happening? A dispute had arisen between the farmers and the agencies of the state on the price of grapes which that year were of very good quality. On the surface it seemed a normal fact of daily life but the Madonna

Vineyards in Medjugorje.

was showing them that by encouraging an obsession on material interests, evil was trying to taking advantage by steering their lives.

Through the years, the Madonna would remind us many times about this ever-present peril in everyday life. The just preoccupation for our daily bread can become an anxious search for human security. If we are not careful, lukewarm faith can lead to the desire for insatiable accumulation of worldly things until God is forgotten. *"Satan — warns the Queen of Peace — wants to sift you through everyday affairs and in your life he wants to snatch the first place."* (Oct. 16/86) Ten years later she is forced to repeat the same warning: *"I invite you again, little children, to put God in the first place in your life. Do not let Satan attract you through material things."* (Mar. 25/96)

When in 1985 the Madonna showed, always more explicitly, her desire to guide us on the way to sanctity, the work of evil stretched out to block the way with trials and temptations in hopes of diverting souls from the holy road: *"Dear children — encourages the Virgin — I love you and therefore, I want you to be holy. I do not want Satan to block you on that way."* (July 25/87) Nothing annoys and worries the evil serpent more than a soul which wants to become a saint, a goal which he tries to oppose in every way: *"Dear children, Satan is strong and is waiting to test each one of you. Pray, and that way he will neither be able to injure you nor block you on the way of holiness."* (Sept. 25/87)

Nevertheless, the enemy doesn't himself block the road which brings us to perfection but tries with infinite sources of seduction to

127

propel us on the way of evil and sin. The verb "to seduce" attributed to Satan, returns numerous times in the heartfelt reminders of the Madonna. On the one hand, he does everything to divert us from the ways of goodness; on the other hand, he pushes us on the road of evil, presenting it as easy and attractive.

Mary understands perfectly in which atmosphere today's world lives, where evil is not only justified but often times even glorified and presented as a good. Man's idea of deciding on his own, what's good and what's bad, is really a subtle trick of evil. In this way it succeeds in leading us as far as possible from the Christian life and God's commandments.

In the consciences of the faithful and most of all in prayer groups, the manner in which Satan operates and attempts to become master of our lives should be clear. Some delude themselves into thinking that his action is limited to disturbing us in external things. Some think he makes attempts on the health of our bodies or our psyche and for this they ask for endless blessings. In reality the enemy aims to hit us more deeply, diverting our hearts from goodness, seducing us with worldly things and compelling us to sin.

A certain superficial way of fighting the tempter which circulates among Christians has always much surprised me. Unfortunately among some, not excluding part of the clergy, there is skepticism, not to say a lack of faith. In many others there is the attitude of superstition which hinders them from seeing the true perils which they face. It has often happened to me to meet people who were prepared to see Satan everywhere except in the moral mediocrity of their lives.

"Dear children — cautions the Madonna — *you are ready to commit sin, and to put yourselves in the hand of Satan without reflecting."* (May 25/87) *"Satan is strong and with all his forces wants to bring the most people possible closer to himself and to sin."* (May 25/95) We wage the true battle against evil when we decide for God and for a holy life. *"Do now allow Satan* — urges the Queen of Peace — *to come into your life through those things that hurt both you and your spiritual life."* (Feb 25/90)

The fight against the enemy is to be waged by an unlimited battle on vice and sin, beginning with our heart. *"Dear children* — cautions our Mother — *do not allow Satan to get control of your hearts, so you would be an image of Satan and not of me."* (Jan. 30/86)

Beside the verb *"to seduce"* we often find repeated the verb *"to destroy."* Only the foolhardy can think that Satan works for our good. Through the things which he offers he wants to take us on the road of ruin and death. His hate and his treachery have no limits. His final objective is to destroy all that is good and holy in us and then to drag us with him in the eternal abyss of everlasting punishment. In the messages of the Queen of Peace, the "poor devil" of popular jargon recaptures the biblical features of viciousness and wickedness.

His devastating violence is focused on the parish, indeed against the entire Church to which he wants to inflict many evils. At the beginning of the Persian Gulf war the Madonna revealed that if God did not restrain him and block his way he would not only destroy human life but even nature and the planet on which we live.

But his destructive action manifests itself in a particular way against the plans of love and peace of God and Mary. *"I am with you — the Madonna reassures us — and I am protecting you even though Satan wishes to destroy my plans and to hinder the desires which the Heavenly Father wants to realize here."* (Sept. 25/90) *"Satan is strong and with all his strength, desires to destroy the peace which comes from God."* (Oct. 25/90) *"Pray, because Satan wants to destroy my plans of peace."* (Dec. 25/90)

While the Madonna was giving these messages, the people were joyful for the soon to be proclaimed independence of Croatia and did not suspect the tremendous danger that the devious serpent was attempting: *"Satan — the Madonna then said — is playing with you and with your souls and I cannot help you because you are far away from my heart."* (March 25/92) *"For now as never before Satan wants to show the world his shameful face by which he wants to seduce as many people as possible onto the way of death and sin."* (Sept. 25/91) *"Satan wants war, wants lack of peace, wants to destroy all which is good."* (March 25/93)

If evil is hiding behind our attachment to material things, to sin and to war, with the purpose of *"stealing as many souls as possible,"* (Oct. 25/92) his presence is no less perilous among the events of ordinary life. He works everywhere to spread lies and division. On the other hand the same word, "devil" means "he who divides." He works in our lives *"through misunderstandings, the non-understanding and non-acceptance of one another."* (Jan. 25/90) *"In these times — the Madonna warns — Satan wants to create disorder in your hearts and in your families."* (Jan. 25/94)

It is not just by accident that the Madonna asked for a year of prayer for families and then another for the young as Vicka often reminds the pilgrims. In fact, in destroying families, he tries to excavate the foundations of society and of the Church. Then he tries to drag the young to himself and destroy their lives using their free time and launching them "onto the bad road."

But then, is Satan so strong that he can *carry [us] about like the branches in the wind*" (May 25/88) and *"do with [us] what he wants,"* (Jan. 25/98) destroying hope in our hearts?

ARM YOURSELVES AGAINST SATAN AND DEFEAT HIM WITH THE ROSARY IN YOUR HANDS

The fact that the Madonna has many times emphasized that *"Satan is strong,"* has always made an impression on me. This assertion perhaps is also the idea which has remained the most etched in the minds of pilgrims. In any battle, but even more in the spiritual realm, the first rule is not to underestimate the adversary. Satan won against our ancestors in the terrestrial paradise, when they were created in a state of grace and sanctity. His shrewdness, his power of deception and his viciousness represent a mortal danger for our souls.

Nevertheless, he was conquered by Jesus and Mary, and with them we can conquer him. In the over fifty messages in which the Madonna puts us on guard against Satan, the weapons with which we can defeat him are always quickly specified. His strength is great if we follow him voluntarily onto the road of sin but he can't do anything if we don't want it.

The Madonna invites us not to be afraid of evil when we experience his perverse activity in our lives. *"God is always watching over us,"* (July 19/97) and he never allows us to be tempted beyond our strength. The real problem, therefore, is our willingness to fight him as we ask for the help of Jesus and of Mary. If we dress in the armaments of light and fight the holy fight, victory is certain, because evil power is a false power.

Unfortunately in many there is passive resignation when confronted with evil. They think that man doesn't have the strength to resist temptation and let themselves be passively dragged on the road to ruin. We are a generation that is not used to battles and sacrifices. Our will has not been trained for denial and we are incapable of saying 'no' to what Satan offers with the intention of making us his and destroying us.

The Mother of God in her long magisterial teachings greatly insists on the formation of the will. The incessant invitation to make small sacrifices and the request for fasting is extremely challenging. The purpose of fasting on bread and water on Wednesdays and Fridays is oriented toward strengthening the will in view of the more important and decisive denial, that of denying sin. Certainly, on our own we would never be able to defeat evil, but if our good will is open to the help of grace, the final victory is assured, even if we have momentary setbacks.

When Satan "battles deceitfully" against us, the Madonna exhorts us to *withstand the days of temptation."* (Jan. 17/85) In the spiritual combat she is always beside us to help us: *"I have stayed with you this long so I might help you along in your trials."* (Feb. 7/85) If we turn to her when we are in danger, Mary will protect us *"with [her] mantle"* (July 11/85). Even in the most desperate situations it is possible to come out winners: *"do not be afraid, because I am with you even if you think there is no way out and that Satan is in control."* (July 25/88)

The only condition necessary to come out victorious is our good will. If it is lacking, God cannot help us. If we do our part, evil will be defeated. *"Without you* — the Queen of Heaven reminds us — *God cannot bring to reality that which He desires. God has given a free will to everyone, and it's in your control."* (Jan. 30/86)

What are the weapons of light with which our good will can be victorious in the holy battle for the eternal salvation of souls? The first weapon is prayer. The Madonna repeats it almost in every message with the triple and intense request now known throughout the world: *"Pray, pray, pray!"*

Prayer in fact calls the power of God to the cause against which the prince of this world can do nothing: *"Only by prayer are you able to overcome every influence of Satan in your place."* (Aug. 7/86) *"If you pray, Satan cannot injure you even a little bit because you are God's children and He is watching over you."* (Feb. 25/88) *"Satan is very strong and, therefore, I ask you to dedicate your prayers to me so that those who are under his influence can be saved."* (Feb. 25/88)

Nevertheless, there is a particularly successful weapon in this battle between heaven and hell and it is the holy rosary. The Madonna has particularly asked for it in Lourdes and in Fatima but in Medjugorje it becomes the decisive weapon for the victorious battle of the Immaculate Heart of Mary: *"Dear children* — exhorts the heavenly guide — *put on the armor for battle and with the Rosary in your hand defeat [Satan]."* (July 8/85) *"Let the rosary always be in your hand as a sign to Satan that you belong to me."* (Feb. 25/88)

In fact the rosary is a humble prayer accessible to all in any moment of the day. It makes present her, who from God has received the mission to crush the head of the serpent. *"With the rosary you shall overcome all the adversities which Satan is trying to inflict on the*

Catholic Church," the Madonna confides to us on the occasion of the anniversary. (June 25/85)

If prayer is the most important weapon for the holy battle, we must not forget the others, no less effective, like sacrifices and denials and in a particular way, fasting: *"Dear children, you are forgetting that I desire sacrifices from you so I can help you and drive Satan away from you."* (Sept. 18/86) In the momentous climax of the war in the former Yugoslavia in which Satan played all his cards to destroy the plans of Mary, the invitation to fasting was absolute: *"Satan is strong and wants to sweep away my plans of peace and joy...Therefore, I call all of you, dear children, to pray and fast still more firmly. I invite you to self-renunciation for nine days [novena] so that, with your help, everything that I desire to realize through the secrets I began in Fatima, may be fulfilled."* (Aug. 25/91)

But this review of the weapons which the Queen of Peace places in our hands would be incomplete unless we refer to something which apparently seems to have little importance. It is a question of blessed objects, like images, statues, icons or pictures which we have in our homes or chains and medals which we carry on ourselves. The Madonna not only approves of them, but recommends them because they are an exterior sign of faith and make the divine blessings present. On this theme the Madonna dedicates an entire message emphasizing its importance: *"Dear children! Today I call you to place more blessed objects in your homes and that everyone put some blessed objects on their person. Bless all the objects and thus Satan will attack you less because you will have armor against him."* (July 18/85)

WITH YOUR HELP I CAN DO EVERYTHING TO FORCE SATAN TO GO AWAY

In September 1986, the Madonna gave a message whose significance I understood only some time later: *"Dear children! Today again I am calling you to prayer and fasting. You know, dear children, that with your help I am able to accomplish everything and force Satan not to be seducing [you] to evil and to remove himself from this place. Dear children, Satan is lurking for each individual. Especially in everyday affairs he wants to spread confusion among each one of you."* (Sept. 4/86) At first sight it can seem only a general teaching without referring to concrete facts. In reality I have been able to verify how often the words of the Madonna throw a light on apparently insignificant daily events.

Just in that week I was in Medjugorje. Marija invited me to participate in Ivan's prayer group and that night Vicka was also there. The place of the reunion was the little room of apparitions in Vicka's maternal home. That night the encounter with the Madonna was exclusively for the members of the group, therefore I waited outside in the corridor. After the rosary and the apparition, the group lingered a long time, talking closely inside closed doors. I asked myself what had happened. Finally the youngsters came out, now in the depth of night, and everyone went home.

I asked Marija if it was possible to know something. She answered that the Madonna had pointed out a house in the village saying that Satan wanted to use it for one of his plans. It concerned a house owned by the community with a large hall which the people in the village used for wedding dinners or other community events. The youngsters of the group had discussed this in depth asking what Satan's plan could be. They did not come to any conclusion but they committed themselves to pray and to fast for this precise intention as the Madonna had asked.

About three months passed when I learned that the Madonna had asked the visionaries to unite the people of the village in the hall of that house to celebrate the novena of Christmas. At the time, the communist regime was pretty strict and forbade any manifestations of religion outside the walls of the churches. Therefore, involvement in the novena by the people was illegal and required a certain dose of courage, because the reaction of the police would certainly not fail.

The novena was happily celebrated with the participation of many people of Bijakovici, in a hall well decorated, with the messages of the Madonna clearly visible on the walls. The people noted the discreet presence of a squad car of the special police every night.

On the eighth day of the novena the Madonna gave the appointment for the concluding day of the novena on the mountain of the first apparitions. When the people came down, they saw the house in question surrounded by a special detachment that was planning a raid. It must be said that in spite of the abundance of stretched nets, they didn't even catch one fish that night.

It all seemed to be over. And Satan's plan? I arrived after the Epiphany and by then the pilgrims had left and the police were taking advantage by interrogating the people. About twenty people were stopped. Even Marija and Vicka were brought to the police station by two brawny police officers. The courage of Vicka struck me greatly on that occasion. She behaved with such calm and at the same time with a determination which came from God. It seemed that we were reliving an episode of the first Christians. The police wanted to know who had organized everything. "The Madonna", answered Vicka. Then turning to the secretary who was transcribing the interrogation, said "Write, and write that it was the Madonna."

Later on I asked the visionaries if the Madonna had made further references to that house. They said no. The discussion, dramatic in the beginning, seemed closed. Evidently the Queen of Peace, with her novena, with the courage of the people and of the visionaries, had received enough to force Satan to leave that house. Sometime later we came to hear that the communist authorities wanted to use the hall of that house, a place exactly at  the foot of the hill of the first apparitions and turn it into a discotheque.

This episode was very instructive for me. More than anything else I was able to understand how Satan behaves hiding in what seem at first to be insignificant daily incidents and also with what weapons the Madonna crushes his head.

CHAPTER 14

Offer your sufferings as gifts to God

WITH BARE FEET ON KRIZEVAC

In Medjugorje there are two mountains full of significance; the first is Podbrdo or Hill of the First Apparitions, the second is Krizevac or Mountain of the Cross called thus because on the top rises a large cement cross built there by the inhabitants of the place in 1933 on the occasion of the 1900 year anniversary of the Redemption. Regarding this cross, the Madonna expressed herself in this way in a very meaningful message: *"The cross was also in God's plan when you built it."* (Aug. 30/84)

The mystery of the cross occupies a fundamental place in Medjugorje. The Madonna often refers to it, especially during Lent. Already on the second day of the apparitions, June 26, 1981, the Queen of Peace appeared in tears to Marija and while she called for reconciliation with God and among men, a dark cross made of wood stood out behind her shoulders. They are the tears of the Mother for the souls of her children who are losing themselves on the road of evil.

An even more concerned reminder was made by the Madonna when on two different occasions she appeared with the suffering Jesus beside her, crowned with thorns, flagellated and dripping blood. On that occasion Jesus was mute and did not even raise His eyes.

I understood how incisive the message of the cross is which comes from Mary during the most beautiful and laborious Way of the Cross of my life. The appointment was for two o'clock in the morning at the foot of Mt. Krizevac. I found myself with Vicka, Sister Elvira and a group of about thirty young people, former drug addicts of the "Campo della Vita" (Camp of Life), one of the numerous communities that this exceptional nun has set up in the world to tear the young from the clutches of drugs and return them to God and to the joy of life.

We began the ascent, stopping for long periods in front of the very beautiful panels of the Stations of the Cross, the work of an Italian sculptor captured by the charm of the Gospa like many other people. Vicka would stop in front of each one, drawing thoughts about suffering from her heart, among the most profound that I had ever heard. The assorted youngsters listened and sang. I had the fortunate idea to record the more significant passages of that Via Crucis (Way of the Cross) which ended when the sun was already high in the sky. I cut out a composition of about two hours that once in a while I have transmitted on Radio Maria by which the listeners are greatly instructed.

Station of the Cross sculpture along Mt. Krizevac.

Vicka would go ahead of us advancing in bare feet on the pointed boulders of the path through the rocks. It is a custom of the place which impresses and often fascinates the pilgrims. Once I observed a young Italian woman who was climbing in bare feet on the last day of the year, oblivious to the polar ice. She told me, smiling, that in this way she wanted to express her love and her thanks to the Madonna.

I saw that Vicka was very taken by the sufferings of Jesus to the point of almost identifying herself with Him. In her spontaneous prayers before the Stations of the Cross she seemed to be reliving the Passion again. Sometimes she referred to Mt. Krizevac as Calvary. By this I understood how much the Madonna had brought the six visionaries into the mystery of the cross.

In the long story recorded at Radio Maria about the apparitions of Medjugorje, Marija Pavlovic affirms that even the visionaries have made their own Via Crucis because of the persecutions of the first years. It is a very fitting assertion. The Madonna has protected her six "angels" but has not saved them from the ordinary crosses of life; indeed, she has added even extraordinary ones, helping them to understand that the cross is of great value. Ivanka had lost her mother at a young age, two months before the beginning of the apparitions. Jakov, who had already lost a father, also lost his mother in the first years of the apparitions. Marija, although delicate of health, had not hesitated to give a kidney to her brother who had no more hope of life.

The grace of seeing the Madonna and the mission to testify about her has become fruitful by means of the cross. The Queen of Peace has first taught the visionaries and then the pilgrims that without the cross, we do not mature in faith.

Concerning understanding the value of suffering, Vicka has lived a very particular experience which should be brought out in the true light. It is not the intention of this work to tell the story of all the events of Medjugorje, not even the most significant. We hope that someone suitable sets about doing this enormous task. Here we are limiting ourselves to pointing out those things which help in the understanding of the message that the Madonna has come to bring. It seems to me that the Queen of Peace has lead Vicka into the mystery of suffering in a particular way.

The spiritual intensity with which she had guided the Via Crucis for many hours had struck me. I understood that this privileged soul was living an authentic mystical experience in relation to the Passion of Jesus. I noticed above all, from some passages of her spontaneous prayers, when with great passion, she exclaimed: "Thank you Jesus, because your cross is grace! Thank you Jesus, because your cross is joy!" She was saying it as if she was experiencing it, as if she was living it in her skin.

In those years Vicka was affected by a mysterious sickness. A bit of everything has been said and written about this. In March 1988 there was a closed door conference in Milan with the participation of about fifteen doctors of various specialties, some of international fame. Even the renowned Marian Mariologist René Laurentin was present. I was also invited to state, as an informed person on these facts, what could have been a key to interpreting a pathology which medicine was not able to decipher.

From time to time, perhaps more or less once a month, Vicka entered into a state of apparent coma, during which she suffered much, not only in her head but in her whole body. I saw her many times in that situation, sometimes awake, other times drowsy while her sisters or some friends helped her. What was it about? Someone in the past had ventured the hypothesis that we were facing a form of hysteria and that even the supposed apparition could be attributed to the same thing. The doctors at the conference, some of whom had studied the phenomenon up close, unanimously excluded a similar hypothesis. Medicine was groping its way in the dark. It was not succeeding in giving a scientific explanation to a phenomenon which was devoid of purely human evaluations.

In my view, the interpretation of that pathology needed to be researched as a particularly mystical experience, not unknown in the story of Christian spirituality. That which commonly was called the state of "coma" was in reality an experience of most intense suffering during which Vicka, even if she externally seemed to be or really was losing her senses, interiorly she was vigilant and in this state of con-sciousness prayed and suffered unspeakably. It could be affirmed that she was reliving interiorly a taste of the Passion of Jesus through the mystical body of the Church.

This situation of mystical suffering which Vicka generally experi-enced for several days lasted for a period of almost four years. In all this time, her life was completely dedicated to the untiring welcoming of the pilgrims which would flock to her house from morning till night, except for these intervals of time in which she was almost taken from the world and made a participant of the sufferings of Jesus.

Who can say what benefits were obtained for the souls who were most in need of graces? This wonderful mystical phenomenon happened in the greatest simplicity and the most rigorous reserve, as if the protago-nist, always smiling, was not aware of it. A few months before, the Madonna announced to Vicka that she would take this suffering away, which was punctually verified on the day which Our Lady had established.

A CHRISTIANITY WITHOUT THE CROSS IS NOT POSSIBLE

Emphasis on the centrality of the cross is typical of the Marian apparitions of Medjugorje. Nothing comparable is found in the message of Lourdes which has become the world centre of the sanctification of suffering. Nor in Fatima, which in recalling sinners to conversion, can be found in line with Medjugorje. What is the reason for this divine strategy? Beside the hill of the first apparitions, she has wanted a small Calvary, while in the flat land, almost at the convergence of the various villages, the great parish church of St. James has risen which receives the faithful for adoration and the Eucharistic sacrifice.

The Madonna sees in the refusal of the cross one of the gravest dangers for the faith today. The modern world doesn't wait for salvation from the cross but on the contrary searches salvation with its own forces. It doesn't seek denial but the confirmation of itself. It doesn't seek salvation by means of suffering but is deceived in thinking it can eliminate pain and one day even death. It doesn't accept the work of the spiritual battle but chases the satisfaction of the desires of the flesh.

The awareness that Christ has suffered for our sins has been obscured even in the conscience of Christians. Indeed, even the perception of the gravity of evil has been extinguished. Fundamental themes like sin and grace, salvation and eternal punishment of souls are avoided in preaching. The presentation of the Mass as the sacrifice of Christ is sometimes put aside in order to emphasize the aspect of a banquet to which many approach without asking themselves if they are in the grace of God.

The Madonna in Medjugorje reminds us that the cross is the heart of faith and that Christianity without the cross is a masquerade. The place chosen for the apparitions is very eloquent. To reach it, the visionaries and the people had to clamber up the mountain, making their way between pointed thorns and sharp rocks, between which venomous snakes would often peek out. In the very concrete teaching methods of the Mother of God, all this was important for the spiritual road along which every Christian is called to travel on the way of Calvary.

The first messages given to the parish and to the world through the visionary Marija indicate with much clarity what is close to the heart of the Mother of God. First, she expresses the desire that all the parishioners be hers, to belong to her Son, Jesus. As to say, like the celebrated expression of Pope Paul VI, that you cannot be Christian if you are not Marian. Secondly, she invites all the parishioners to conversion so that they can help all those who come to Medjugorje to convert. Thirdly, she urges the adoration of the Blessed Sacrament without interruption. Fourthly, the Madonna taking the starting point of the beginning of Lent, begins that catechesis on the Passion which is one of the leading themes of her teaching.

"Dear children! In a special way this evening I am calling you during Lent to honour the wounds of my Son, which He received from the sins of this parish. Unite yourselves with my prayers for the parish so that His sufferings may be bearable." (March 22/84) In this message the reminder of the reality of Christ's passion strikes us. He has not only suffered in the past but suffers today and not for some anonymous sins but for those very concrete sins which the parishioners commit every day. He is crucified today for your and my sins. This is why, as Pascal said, Jesus is in agony until the end of the world.

In a succeeding message the Madonna reminds us of that tradition, still alive in Christian people, of the heart of Jesus which is offended by the sins and ingratitude of men. She desires to make this tradition alive and real: *"Dear children! This evening I pray you especially to venerate the Heart of my Son, Jesus. Make reparation for the wound inflicted on the Heart of my Son. That Heart is offended by all kinds of sins."* (April 5/84) The Madonna not only reminds us that grave sin exists, something which sometimes is passed over by our superficial catechesis, but reveals its profound malice: it is a lack of love, even to becoming refusal and contempt for the love of He who gave His life for us.

So many offenses and so much ingratitude demand reparation. Here is the invitation to *"honour the wounds"* and to *"honour the heart."* Then it is necessary to offer sacrifices, acts of love, so that the sufferings of Christ are eased: *"Dear children! In a special way this evening I am calling you to perseverance in trials. Consider how the Almighty is still suffering today on account of your sins. So when sufferings come, offer them up as a sacrifice to God."* (March 29/84)

Near the heart of Jesus we quickly find the heart of Mary. It is the heart of the Mother to which all men have been entrusted like children, and that she loves equally, even when they are far from her and from her Son and on the road to sin. *"Please* — pleads the sorrowful Virgin — *do not let my heart weep with tears of blood because of the souls who are lost in sin."* (May 24/84) This is the profound reason for the tears of blood which fall from the eyes of the Madonna. It is a question of the greatest irreparable disaster: the everlasting punishment and loss of a soul.

We see combined in the call of Mary in Medjugorje the great tradition of the Heart of Jesus, inaugurated by St. Mary Margaret Alacoque and that of the Immaculate Heart of Mary spread by Sister Lucia of Fatima. We know how these two currents of spirituality are connected by the practices of the first nine Fridays and the first five Saturdays of the month. To each is bound the special divine promise to receive the gift and grace of final perseverance and eternal salvation of the soul. In this way the Queen of Peace manifests God's great plan which she is bringing forward in Medjugorje; it is a question of rescuing all the souls for whom Christ has spilled His blood from evil, and to deliver them to God *"like a stupendous flower for eternity."*

This pedagogy of the cross certainly has its end point when on two occasions the Madonna appeared with the suffering Jesus beside her. This happened once on Good Friday. On another occasion, as the visionary Marija has retold in an interview at Radio Maria, it was to encourage the youngsters and the parish that were particularly persecuted by the police in those days. The Madonna, showing Jesus, said: *"I want you to see how much Jesus has suffered for you."* Even after many years I have noticed that both Vicka and Marija retell this episode with great emotion.

The crude realism of the vision of Christ's sufferings for our sins has left deep traces in the visionaries even after many years have passed. From their testimony comes a message that is the heart of the Gospel itself. Our salvation has cost the blood of the Son of God. He not only suffered then, but suffers today for the sins of men. What executioners did to Him continues until the end of the world because of the actions of all sinners. As He accepted the relief of human pity owing to the presence of the few good who were following Him on the way of the cross, so now He seeks the comfort of our love and our atonement.

Mary in Medjugorje reminds us that Good Friday is the heart of the human story. In fact, on that day the redemption of the world occurred. In vain men would search for salvation elsewhere. Salvation comes from the cross and from the participation in the sufferings of the Crucified One.

GREAT GRACES COME FROM THE CROSS

In a certain sense this spirituality of the cross which is possible to develop beginning from the messages of the Queen of Peace is counter-cultural. It is a question of the concrete lessons that Mary gives to whoever is carrying the cross of persecution, of trials, of temptation, of solitude, of destitution and of sickness. She sees the crosses which the parish carries and which are on the shoulders of the pilgrims who arrive in Medjugorje searching for some relief. To a society that doesn't know how to carry the cross of life and that has forgotten that every man is born crucified, the Madonna reminds us of the teaching of Jesus: "If anyone wants to be a follower of mine, let him deny himself and take up his cross every day and follow me." (Luke 9,23)

We live in a crucified world but which would like to come down from the cross. Today mankind does not like to carry the cross. Even Christians look more for the grace of healing than for endurance. The Madonna shows us Jesus crucified and she asks us to contemplate Him. Then we will understand that the way of the cross is not only grace but also joy, real joy, which is already a foreshadowing on this earth of the joy of heaven.

Numerous are the refrains to *"pray before the cross"* and *"meditate on the passion."* The crucifix should again have a place of honour in our churches and even in our homes. Is it not true that one of the attacks on Christianity today is evidenced by means of the elimination of crucifixes from public places? Some have even come to insist that the crucifix in schools would have negative consequences on the psychology of children. We cannot allow the superficial and even irritating way in which crucifixes today are commercialized and fashionably used to pass unobserved. And yet what symbol could better represent the human condition so in need of salvation?

The Madonna even goes so far as to recommend to *"make a special consecration to the cross"* in our homes. (Sept. 12/85) What does it mean? It means a spirituality of the cross which needs to be at the centre of the Christian life. It is made up of meditation on the Passion, of prayer kneeling before the cross but also of making amends and participating in the sufferings of Jesus. The Madonna in fact wants us to

promise to *"neither offend Jesus nor abuse the cross."* (Sept. 12/85) Then she also invites us *"to accept sickness and suffering with love the way Jesus accepted them."* (Sept. 11/86) The goal in our crucified life is being united to the crucified Jesus. (Feb. 20/86)

I have to say, even from a personal experience, that nature rebels at the cross. It is useless to hide it; the cross frightens us. It has a multitude of ways of expressing its existence. There is a labour to living which is on the skin of us all. There are not only the physical crosses which sooner or later everyone encounters. Who is exempt from sickness, from old age, from death? Moreover, there are emotional crosses which are even harder to carry. Who can understand what it means for a mother to lose a son? Then there are the moral crosses, like incomprehension, persecution, injustice, solitude which break even the most strengthened souls. Finally, there are the spiritual crosses of those who have lost the reason to live, their self esteem and the hope of saving themselves and fear of hurtling into the gloomy abyss of desperation.

Humanity is crucified but it's like the two thieves beside Jesus. Either he looks at Jesus and finds the key to suffering or he dies cursing and damning. In any case, no one can come down from the cross. It cannot be eliminated. Either you accept it and offer it up, or it crushes and destroys you. The Son of God died on the cross to redeem our crosses. The Madonna affirms this with much resolution: to the cross come great graces. What graces?

From the cross first of all comes forgiveness of sins. Existence without God is perhaps the most terrible of sufferings. Separated from Him we wander around without direction, without ideals, without motivations and, most of all, without love in life. St. Catherine of Siena is correct when, with expressive daring, affirms that "the martyrs of hell" exist. They are those who have lost God and with Him light, truth, beauty and joy. Victims of remorse, how could they be freed if not by throwing themselves on their knees before Jesus crucified and asking for total pardon, free and unaffected by the evil they have done?

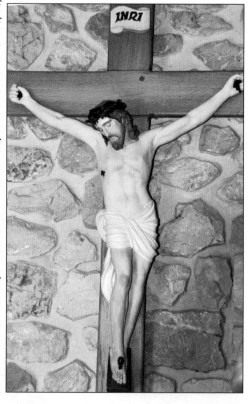

Among the great graces which come from the cross, the first and the most important is that of conversion, because Christ suffered for our sins. But if we offer Jesus all the other crosses of life, the physical, emotional, moral and spiritual, they are transformed into something positive. And in union with the cross of Christ they become the strength of salvation for us and for others. Jesus gives meaning to our cross, unites it to His, making it lighter and even transforming it into joy.

If accepted from the hands of God with love, the cross is grace. This is the message which comes to us from the Queen of Peace. Personally I have had this unique experience in Medjugorje, which I want to communicate because it seems to be a teaching method which God often uses with souls. Before granting special graces God always asks for something. Often it is a question of accepting with love some physical pain and other small sufferings. If you make the heartfelt efforts to say your 'yes,' God will give you an overabundance of what was proposed.

It is not necessary to look for sufferings. Human life is already crucified. Welcome with total acceptance whatever God sends you through daily events. Accept them and offer them to Christ. Make an effort of the heart and show Jesus that you want to alleviate His pain with your small pain. Then you will understand what it means that the cross is grace and that the cross is joy.

Is it perhaps wrong to ask God to take away our suffering, especially the physical? The Madonna gives a very profound lesson about this: *"Dear children, pray that you may be able to accept sickness and suffering with love the way Jesus accepted them. Only that way shall I be able with joy to give out to you the graces and healings which Jesus is permitting me."* (Sept. 11/86) The Madonna asks you to first accept so that you put her in a position to be able to bless you. Know, however, that if she leaves you with your sickness or your suffering, she has perhaps given you a greater grace.

Diana Basile of Milan, one of the numerous persons who were healed in Medjugorje, recovered perfectly from a sclerosis on her skin. One day during a public testimony she said: "I am grateful to the Madonna for my healing but I miss my disease." She had understood that the sufferings offered like a gift to God become *"a most beautiful flower of joy."* (Sept. 25/96)

CHAPTER 15

"Peace, peace, peace!"

A WORLD WITHOUT PEACE

In the various presentations of the principal messages of the Madonna in Medjugorje, peace is last, following faith, prayer, fasting and conversion. In reality there is a very wise logic in this artificial list for catechetical use. The road of faith in fact, fed by prayer and denial, brings us to conversion and a return to God. The final goal is divine peace in our hearts which is one of the greatest gifts that the Creator could give on this earth, at least for those who have experienced it.

In the first years that I was going to Medjugorje, I had not grasped the scope of the message regarding peace because as I understood later, the Madonna gave to this expression a different significance than what is commonly used. It was on a particular occasion while I was helping Vicka to receive pilgrims on that little stair of her house now known all over the world, that I had the intuition of the greatness of the message of peace.

An American pilgrim asked Vicka which, according to her, was the most important of the messages. To my great surprise, Vicka answered that the one she felt the most, from a personal experience, was the message of peace. Saying this she placed her hand on her heart and with a big smile pointed out the sweetness of which the human heart is overflowing when it is at peace with God. I understood on that occasion that the peace of which we humans speak, is only the echo of a more profound reality that only God can give to whoever opens his heart to Him.

Many have experienced the peace that the Madonna invites us to in the sacrament of reconciliation. It is the pardon of God which descends like an ointment of healing on the wounds and on the shame of a life marked by evil. In the long lines of pilgrims who wait before the confessionals in Medjugorje, you see the seekers of that peace that the world cannot give and does not even know. You see it flowing along cheeks bathed in tears of repentance which then transform the faces into those of joy. The priestly absolution which frees the contrite heart from sin permits us to taste the divine peace of paradise already on this earth.

It cannot be denied that in the last few decades, men have multiplied their efforts to avoid the experience of a new world war, which with the lethal arms at their disposal would have destroyed the earth and all its inhabitants. We have passed from the balancing act of the Cold War years to those involving international treaties for atomic disarmament. But while men were deluding themselves to have reached "peace and security," the Queen of Peace appeared in tears already on the second day of the apparitions imploring: *"Peace, peace, peace and only peace."* (June 25/81) Then still in tears, she added twice: *"Peace has to reign between God and man and among men."* [4]

Perhaps we have not meditated enough on the fact that, while men thought that they had pacified the world, the Madonna in Medjugorje presented herself as Queen of Peace in *"a world without peace."* This expression recurs often in the messages. The Mother of God does not look at the paper treaties but the hearts of men in which divine peace does not yet live.

On what basis can peace reign when in man's heart there is pride, egoism, indifference, greed, persecution and violence? Can a world which delivers itself into the hands of evil live serenely? Will not he who is a liar and a murderer from the beginning not bring the world first to desperation and then to destruction?

Mary in Medjugorje has put us on guard against illusion and false optimism. International treaties alone do not guarantee the future of peoples. Without the changing of hearts, blind hate becomes a force of unstoppable destruction. The three and a half years of war in the Balkan countries where the Queen of Peace is appearing have demonstrated to what unthinkable limits of cruelty the human heart can arrive.

Civil wars in different countries seem in these last years to have replaced the conflicts between the super powers. They are even more lethal as shown by the horrendous massacres committed in numerous parts of the world from Rwanda to Algeria. Without the return of humanity to the God of love, peace is impossible.

Peace is the fruit of all the messages that the Madonna has given in Medjugorje. She sees the world the way it is in reality before God. It is a proud world which presumes to construct itself without God and which looks to riches and power for the reason to live and to act. For this restless world there is neither a future nor eternal salvation.

In order for humanity to enter a time of peace which the heart of Mary *"waits impatiently for,"* (June 25/95) it is necessary to travel the road of conversion and return to God. In fact, only when men have made peace with God, returning to being His sons, will they be able to recognize each other as brothers. Any attempt to realize peace without God is destined to failure. If the Lord does not build the house, the builders work in vain.

"Dear children — warns the Madonna a few months before the flare-up of war — *Today, I invite you to decide for God, because distance from God is the fruit of the lack of peace in your hearts. God is only peace. Therefore, approach Him through your personal prayer and then live peace in your hearts and in this way peace will flow from your hearts like a river into the whole world. Do not talk about peace, but make peace."* (Feb. 25/91)

Who does not remember with what sadness Mary spurred us on to prayer and fasting during the years of tremendous conflict? *"Only by prayer and fasting can war be stopped,"* (April 25/92) she affirmed in one of the more troubled moments of the conflict when Satan was looking *"to seduce as many souls as possible."* (April 25/92) In those months I remember a group of hundreds of Italians trying to go to Sarajevo which was surrounded by opposing armies, to testify for peace.

Was this march necessary? I was wondering that myself when the organizers asked me to publicize it using the microphones of Radio Maria. I was hesitant until I exchanged a few words with Mons. Tonino Bello, one of the organizers of the march along with Mons. Bettazzi. We were in the heart of winter. These men had decided to proceed in the midst of ice, hunger, misery and danger, to bring the message of peace and joy to Sarajevo.

Mons. Bello struck me greatly while I was talking to him before the interview. He didn't seem to be a bishop, as his way of presenting himself was so bashful and humble. He was already suffering, sapped by a tumor which would have brought him to heaven. He spoke with humility but at the same time with fervour and the zeal of a real servant of God.

I had prepared one of my objections: "Monsignor — I wanted to say — it seems that prayer is needed more than marches." But then I didn't say anything. I invited him to speak without fear about the march for peace in the studios of Radio Maria. I had understood that he was living the message of Mary to be *"carriers of peace and of God's joy to today's world without peace,"* (Oct 25/97) more than we were. I also understood that the march, which carried the risk of death, was the expression of the highest form of prayer and fasting.

The Madonna has guided the parish in the dark period of war, asking for prayers, fasting, sacrifices and an increase of love. At the end she gave thanks for the help received to crush the head of the serpent of hate and of ethnic cleansing: *"Dear children!*

War-damaged Mostar Cathedral.

Today I thank you for your prayers. All of you have helped me so that this war may end as soon as possible. I am close to you and I pray for each one of you and I beg you: pray, pray, pray. Only through prayer can we defeat evil and protect all that Satan wants to destroy in your lives." (Feb. 25/94)

Why has it been possible to put an end to the war with prayer? The profound reason is to look into the roots of the war itself, which lives in the heart that sees an adversary in his brother. In order for that look to change and for the enemy to become a friend it is necessary that the love of the heavenly Father enters our hearts. Then the one you wanted to annihilate becomes a brother to embrace. But this is possible only if in prayer one experiences the love with which God loves all men infinitely and without exception.

A world without God and without prayer is inevitably a world without love and without peace. For this world there is no future but only the specter of self destruction. But if man returns to God and experiences His peace, then the future will see the civilization of love.

GOD ALLOWS ME TO ACHIEVE THIS
OASIS OF PEACE WITH HIM

My impression is that we Christians have not yet understood the evangelical message of peace in all its immensity. When we speak of peace our thoughts instinctively go to those parts of the world where there is war. We almost never stop to think about our hearts which are often not at peace either with ourselves, our neighbor or with God. A man at peace strikes you at first sight. You see the light in his eyes, the tranquility in his soul, and his humble welcome. He is serene, available, optimistic and even joyful. The storms of life ripple the waves superficially but do not disturb the deep peace.

There is nothing greater than the peace of God. It is the beginning of paradise. When she describes the divine life, the Madonna says that in heaven there is peace and joy. These two expressions are frequently used together in her messages. Well then, her desire and her program are that the peace and joy of God be poured again in our hearts to fill them to the brim so we can then give them to those who have none.

In this intention Mary places herself in the deep furrow of the evangelical message. When did the announcement of divine peace ring out for the first time in heaven? Is it not perhaps on Christmas night when Jesus came into the world? And is not the first greeting of the Risen Christ, victorious over evil, addressed to the apostles hidden in the cenacle, that of peace? Divine peace is the fruit of redemption. It is the fundamental announcement of Christmas and of Easter.

Mary in Medjugorje wants to give us something so essential without which it is impossible to live. If at Lourdes she presented herself as the Immaculate Conception and at Fatima as the Madonna of the Rosary, in Medjugorje the name of Mary is "Queen of Peace." This is how she called herself from the beginning, and already on the third day of the apparitions she had given her principal message in tears.

Many times she will repeat that this is the program she has received from God, especially on the occasion of the feast of Christmas: *"Dear children! I call you to peace. Live it in your heart and all around you, so that all will know peace, peace that does not come from you but from God. Little children, today is a great day. Rejoice with me. Glorify the Nativity of Jesus through the peace that I give you. It is for this peace that I have come as your Mother, Queen of Peace."* (Dec. 25/88)

The real problem is that of understanding, indeed of experiencing what is divine peace. It is the heart overflowing with the love of God. When we have no love we are restless. We search for it but we are not in peace. When love satisfies us, and this is possible only with divine love, then we feel at peace and we are overflowing with joy. Heaven is already present in us as a deposit, according to the expression of St. Paul.

All the messages of the Mother of God in Medjugorje are summarized in this objective. Faith, prayer, repentance, conversion is the beginning of the road to sanctity which brings us, even in this life, to taste divine peace and joy. This is what the human heart desires and to search elsewhere is in vain. All those who have let themselves be guided by the Madonna know that true happiness is not a fantasy and it is possible to experience it already in this life by carrying our crosses every day.

To realize her plan to *"Let peace reign in the whole world,"* (July 25/90) the Madonna wants to build in Medjugorje *"an oasis of peace."* (Aug 7/86) This expression has struck the followers of the Gospa greatly even if it hasn't yet been understood in all its depth. Even a religious family which carries this name has been born. Let's not have any illusions. Before the apparitions, Medjugorje wasn't any better than many other parishes of Christianity. It was also part of this troubled world and without peace.

God has mysteriously selected this little piece of ground to make an oasis of peace from which divine peace could spread to all the world. The Madonna announces this heavenly project, calling the parishioners to co-operate: *"Dear children! God is allowing me along with Himself to bring about this oasis of peace. I wish to call on you to protect it and that the oasis always be unspoiled. There are those who by their carelessness are destroying the peace and the prayer. I am inviting you to give witness and by your own life to help to preserve the peace."* (June 26/86)

With infinite patience the Queen of Peace places her hand on her project. First of all, it is necessary that there be reconciliation with God. In this way the insistent invitation to confession gains its real value. It is first a question of finding divine friendship, otherwise any effort is useless: *"You cannot, little children, realize peace if your are not at peace with Jesus. Therefore, I invite you to confession so Jesus may be your truth and peace."* (Jan. 25/95)

The Madonna has certainly succeeded in the course of the years to engrave this in our hearts and to build what she desired, even considering the relative limitation of the human condition. In fact, whoever arrives in Medjugorje truly breathes, even if unaware, a climate of peace that is difficult to experience elsewhere. This was happening even in the first years when the communist regime controlled and tried to irritate the population.

Many times I have asked myself what Medjugorje has that is so extraordinary. Apparently nothing. And yet, as soon as you arrive, you enter into a spiritual atmosphere of great peacefulness, as if the Madonna was wrapping the great basin surrounded by the circle of mountains, into her cloak. The name of Medjugorje means "between the mountains." The Madonna has wanted to make of this village a beautiful flower brimming with God so that all who come there can smell the perfume of heavenly peace.

I have noted that many pilgrims want to return there. Some have gone to Medjugorje dozens and dozens of times. This rarely happens with other holy places. What does the secret call have that is so difficult to resist? Without a doubt it is the presence of that divine peace which the human heart desires even though it is often unaware of it. The people are happy to stay in Medjugorje. When they return to their homes they speak of it with longing. There they have experienced what is difficult to find anywhere else. In this place the Queen of Peace leaves the fragrance of the heavenly beatitudes in a special way.

Even entering into the families you notice this climate. The Slavs in general and the Croatians in particular have a rather excitable and aggressive temperament. The Madonna has known how to perfect them in the course of the years. In the first periods of the apparitions she had warned the visionaries that Satan was trying to worm his way among them. It is marvelous how these six very different young people have been able to maintain themselves as a close and harmonious group. When it has been necessary, the Madonna has intervened to preserve the parish from the divisions and the quarrels sown by the devil: *"Dear children* — she cautions — *today I beseech you to stop slandering and to pray for the unity of the parish, because I and my Son have a special plan for this parish."* (April 12/84)

Numerous are the reminders to reconciliation in families and reciprocal forgiveness. Let us not delude ourselves: even in Medjugorje there are those who, as the Madonna says, *"with their indifference annihilate peace and prayer."* There isn't a field of wheat where the enemy doesn't scatter his weeds. The Madonna warns of the danger: *"Dear*

152

children — she says — *You know that I promised you an oasis of peace, but you don't know that beside an oasis stands the desert, where Satan is lurking and wanting to tempt each one of you.*" (Aug. 7/86)

In spite of this, it can be said that Mary's plan to construct in Medjugorje a foundation of what will be the future civilization of love, has been fulfilled. Thinking about it, the real fascination of Medjugorje, which will not diminish even with the end of the apparitions, lives just in this divine project.

In the war years which raged especially in Bosnia-Herzegovina, Medjugorje did not lose its characteristic of "oasis of peace." The pilgrims never diminished but most of all prayer was never lacking. On the occasion of some festivals, I have seen hundreds of motor vehicles from every part of Europe, particularly from Italy, full of assistance for the people of whatever ethnic group they belonged. Never as in those years was prayer so intimately joined to charity.

In that very difficult time the visionary who more than others remained on the spot in Medjugorje was Vicka. The war was a hard necessity from which you couldn't escape. Even Vicka's three brothers had to respond to the call to arms. I have often talked with them to learn about the situation up close. The seriousness of their attitude has always impressed me. It was a question in substance of doing everything necessary to defend their villages and their country without useless violence and wanting a general reconciliation as soon as possible.

A cluster bomb that did not detonate during the war in 1992. The villagers 'planted' it in a sewer drain outside St. James Church.

In the more than three years of a very difficult conflict, Vicka distinguished herself by her tireless presence, not only in receiving the pilgrims, but also and above all, in helping the wounded and the sick, in distributing assistance and comfort to the soldiers. She worked wonders so that they would go to the frontlines of the fighting reconciled with God, after having received the sacraments of confession and communion.

During the war, Medjugorje appeared like a miracle of prayer and charity which the Queen of Peace placed before the eyes of the world. She gave a sign of her presence that only the blind didn't want to see. The nearby city of Mostar, only twenty kilometers away as the crow flies, was almost entirely destroyed. In particular, the cathedral and the Franciscan convent were demolished by the bombs.

The Serbs from the hills around Mostar had cannons and rocket launchers pointed at the church with the two bell towers [Medjugorje]. There were no illusions. Who can count the number of Catholic churches systematically destroyed in those years?

The objective of the Serbian army was to reduce Medjugorje to a pile of rubble. Let's not forget that Croatia had proclaimed its independence, separating from the Yugoslavian federation, exactly on June 25, 1991, the tenth anniversary of the apparitions. To strike and to destroy this religious symbol was a priority objective for the Serbs in order to weaken the morale of the Croatians.

I remember in those days many who questioned me on the course of the war in Bosnia. When they asked about Medjugorje they were very surprised that it hadn't been hit yet. There was a kind of silent waiting in international public opinion. "Let's see if he comes down from the cross" the enemies of Jesus were saying, making fun of Him. "Let's see if the Madonna will save Medjugorje" suggested the stubborn enemies of the apparitions, perhaps more numerous than one thinks.

One morning I found myself as usual at the bookstall to buy the newspapers for my daily program of comments on the news. To my astonishment and pain I saw that the newspapers were reporting with evidence that Medjugorje had been bombarded. Even the Catholic newspaper Avvenire which for cautious reasons almost never touched this subject, published the article on the first page. I thought the event possible because the ways of God are not our ways, but in my personal feelings I didn't think it possible.

I picked up the telephone and called Vicka's family. Miraculously I was quickly connected in spite of the almost impossibility of communicating by telephone in those war years. Her mother answered and I put her directly on the microphones of Radio Maria. The tranquility of her voice, even if she was speaking in Croatian, persuaded our public that the situation was not so catastrophic. I asked her about news of the bombardments. That morning the Italians of Medjugorje, dazed by the news in the newspapers and television, learned that effectively the bombardment had happened. A few Serbian devices fired from the hills very near Mostar had flown over the two bell towers and had exploded in a field, killing a poor cow. Satan had not achieved any more.

I INVITE YOU TO HELP EVERYONE WITH YOUR PEACE

Divine peace of the heart is the end goal of all the messages of Medjugorje. Whoever has it already experiences the beatitudes of heaven during our earthly pilgrimage. The Madonna wants to bring us all to paradise with her. She desires that we smell its fragrance already here on earth so that we don't lose the way which leads to the heart of Trinitarian love. Mary's project is for men to taste, already in this life, the peace that God wants to pour again into their hearts.

To present Medjugorje as an ominous event would be to lead people astray. I have heard the seers affirm many times that the Madonna has not come to frighten us. Some make improper references to the "secrets" presenting the future in apocalyptic colours. In reality the Madonna has come as the Queen of Peace and hers are projects of goodness for the entire world.

Medjugorje is a transcendent design of the merciful love of God as it has perhaps never been manifested in the Christian story. Not accidentally has this become real and is connected to a pontificate of a very clear Marian stamp. This Marian quality is among the most significant that the Church has known. We don't need to mistake the smallness of the means and the insignificance of the characters on the world stage. God has always accomplished great deeds which have changed humanity with instruments hardly visible to the world.

The Madonna has never hidden the splendour of the plan in which each of us has an important place (Jan.25/87) and she invites us *"to build a new world of peace with [her]."* (Dec. 12/92) Could a project be more ambitious? No one more than Mary is aware of the difficult situation of the world in which *"there is a great lack of peace."* But because she is our Mother and she loves us, she doesn't want to leave us in this situation in which men are without God, without love, without joy, without a future and without eternal salvation.

In the first phase of her plan the Madonna has begun to build "an oasis of peace" where men, through the reawakening of faith, the zeal of prayer and the changing of lives would begin to taste the sweetness of divine peace in their hearts. Subsequently she has abundantly filled the hearts of the pilgrims coming from every part of the world with the tenderness of a Mother. This is so they could experience in this heavenly oasis how good and gentle is the Lord. Finally, with those who are now hers and are full of her maternal love, she wants to bring the gentleness of the love of God to all men.

How many times, especially in these last years, have we heard her heartfelt appeal *"Dear children, I love you and I desire to bring all of you to the peace which only God gives and which enriches every heart. I invite you to become carriers and witnesses of my peace to this unpeaceful world."* (July 25/90) *"I invite you to be apostles of love and goodness. In this world of unrest give witness to God and God's love, and God will bless you and give you what you seek from Him."* (Oct. 25/93) *"I desire for you to become carriers of peace and of God's joy to today's world without peace."* (Oct. 25/97)

What do we need to wait for in the future? If we help the Queen of Peace put her plan into action, giving our restless and desperate brothers the peace, joy and love which God pours into our hearts, there isn't any doubt that soon a time of peace which the heart of Mary *"waits impatiently for"* (June 25/95) will come on the earth. If we will participate, a great dream could soon become reality!

CHAPTER 16

Dear young people

EVERYTHING THAT THE WORLD OFFERS YOU TODAY IS PASSING

There is no doubt that the apparitions of Medjugorje have a special summons for the young. In a different way from other Marian shrines, the presence of the young here quickly strikes you. They arrive from every part of the world, often like hungry dogs searching for a shred of the Absolute. Some remain in Medjugorje for several months like those who are ill and need time to recuperate their energies to restart their journey.

Certainly, many among them are believers but it is an uncertain and wavering faith. It needs a live encounter to almost touch God with their hands in order to obtain strength to confront the future. Others are simply defeated in life. They are in a desperate search for reasons to live and to believe, having themselves experienced in their own skin the bitterness and emptiness of their own lives.

I have discovered in Medjugorje the extraordinary attraction of Mary on the young. It almost seems that they see her and they feel her beauty and the tenderness of her motherly gaze. Some of the most beautiful Marian songs were born out of the desire of the young to sing the praises of the Queen of Peace. Here innumerable lives are radically changed. Many parents, very much surprised, have seen their children return home profoundly transformed.

The young are a constant presence, spread out throughout the year. Medjugorje is very hospitable. Even the most disoriented can find a family where they can stay. There is no lack of organization for receiving them where they can have a point of reference for the spiritual journey.

The Madonna wished for her birthday to be celebrated on August 5. The preceding week sees tens of thousands of young people from every part of the world congregating to celebrate the Youth Festival under the mantle of the Queen of Peace.

These unforgettable experiences mark our existence. Often a pilgrimage to Medjugorje has inspired the heart of a young person more than many years of catechesis in the parish. The presence of Mary is real and the young understand that Christianity is something concrete which is engraved into your life and makes it great. Here many of them have heard the call for a total consecration to the service of God and the Church.

The undeniable fascination which Medjugorje exercises on the young finds its explanation in the particular concern of the Queen of Peace for the youth. We must not forget that in contrast to many other Marian apparitions, here Mary has not chosen children but teenagers who were facing the difficult years of growth. With the exception of Jakov, who at the time of the first apparition was only ten years old, all the rest were from fifteen to seventeen years of age.

The Madonna chose them just at the moment when their contemporaries often abandon God and the Church to follow roads full of perils and deadly dangers. Through them Mary has wanted to become the Mother and the guide of the world's young people. These are youngsters who in many cases have been abandoned to themselves, without mother or father, and deprived of real teachers of life. The six visionaries of Medjugorje are a sign of the maternal preoccupation of Mary for a generation which runs the risk of losing the torch of faith handed down by the Church.

International Youth Festival in Medjugorje.

I have been able to hear some particular messages of the Madonna for the young from Ivan and Vicka. Ivan conducts a prayer group consisting of his peers. The Queen of Peace has guided and formed them from the first years of the apparitions. Ivan preserves all the messages with which the Virgin has accompanied the group. Perhaps one day, through them, we will be able to better understand her divine wisdom in teaching the young the way of faith.

Perhaps the most noted words of the Madonna regarding the young are those which Vicka includes in her effective synthesis of the messages, with which she regularly addresses the pilgrims. The Gospa advises by affirming that the young today *"find themselves in a very difficult situation."* What does it mean? The Madonna does not say it explicitly, but we can get an idea from the totality of her messages.

Vicka

Above all the Mother is very concerned for the crisis in the family. In many cases the parents have abandoned their duty to teach the faith and the children have fallen away without knowing God and the way of goodness. Graver still is the situation of the young in divided families who then must confront those decisive years without the guidance of their parents, and abandoned to themselves morally and emotionally.

The Madonna sees the young and families as a unique problem. In fact, after having dedicated a year to prayer for the young, she asked for another year of prayer together for youth and families. Mary knows very well that the family plays a decisive role in the life of a young person, in good as in evil. The crisis of many families places the young in gravely difficult situation and is the first reason they lose their way.

Nevertheless many young people, even having received a good religious education from their parents, end up finding themselves in difficulty because of the general situation of society. On many occasions the Queen of Peace affirms that *"sin dominates"* the world and humanity *"walks in darkness,"* deceiving itself in building *"a future without God."* The result is that men get lost along the road of evil and are unhappy and without peace.

In this emptiness of values and of ideals, how can the young discover *"the greatness and joy of life?"* (Mar 29/89) We shouldn't be surprised if a large part of contemporary youth doesn't know what to do with its own existence and tries to fill the chasm of emptiness with the "idols" of the moment.

"Dear young people — says the Madonna addressing them directly in the message referred to before, given through Vicka — *everything that today's world offers you is passing."* Here Mary puts her finger on the wound and calls our entire generation to order. In fact, what are we offering our youth? This question is directed both to families as well as to society.

There is no doubt that our primary preoccupation is not letting our children miss out on anything materially. We nourish their bodies, but not their souls. Rarely do they hear words from us that enter their hearts. The consumer society aggravates this situation, seducing them with the diabolic lie of instant happiness. Once out of the house, what do our young people seek? Many lose themselves after money and enjoyment. Many destroy themselves in the search for artificial paradise. A large part of our children are walking dead. The absence of God has deprived them of life, joy and hope.

The Madonna wants above all to help the young to become aware of the Satanic deception. The momentary things pass. They cannot give a sense to life and produce happiness. "Whoever drinks from this water will still be thirsty," Jesus says with His penetrating style which does not allow replication. It is not with the deceptive allurements of the world that man can satisfy his heart's hunger for eternity. The young, more than any other, are ready to pursue the false happiness which society exhibits, and then perish with hunger and boredom.

"SATAN WANTS TO USE YOUR FREE TIME TO HIS ADVANTAGE"

The deceptive action of the serpent hides behind the transient things that the world offers. Mary is a mother, indeed in Medjugorje she is the mother of the young in a totally special way. Therefore we shouldn't be surprised if she comes into the tangible world to warn her children the dangers they are risking: *"Satan* — she says — *wants to use your free time to his advantage."* Such a relevant reference to a precise situation of life in which our youngsters find themselves has always impressed me greatly.

In fact, until a young person is busy with studies or with work, it is more difficult for him to surrender to any grave detours. The work of seduction begins with free time which of itself isn't something negative but the eternal liar sees the opportunity to unfold his work of seduction. What do our young people do in their free time? In one message the Madonna invited everyone to go to nature. Therefore there is also a positive way to use moments of liberty to strengthen ourselves in body and spirit.

Free time however, becomes a Satanic opportunity when it is used to damage the body and the soul. Everything which is diabolical has the appearance of good but in reality it impoverishes us, empties us and destroys us. It isn't difficult to identify in the discotheques, in drugs, in free sex and in easy money the instruments with which Satan becomes proprietor of our youngsters' lives to bring them to ruin.

I would like to reflect for a moment on the discotheque, regarding the many voices which unfortunately minimize its negative effects. As combined statistics demonstrate, the discotheque is the place in which many youngsters drug themselves, beginning that work of demolition which takes them to becoming walking cadavers. But even when it doesn't lead to drugs, the discotheque equally manifests its poisonous work with music which mesmerizes, with alcohol which intoxicates and sex which is degraded to an impulse.

It is something to reflect that for a third of Italian youngsters, the discotheque is the reason for life itself, which makes sense of their week and without which they wouldn't be able to live. The Satanic deception is perfect in which he who is "murderer and liar from the beginning" has enclosed a large part of our young people in these immense rooms of chatter, fooling them that they are in paradise. Is it not interesting that many discotheques have just this name? But there is no doubt that in these Satanic paradises you can quite quickly smell the odour of sulfur, emptiness, unhappiness and desperation.

How is it possible not to see the trap of the demon in the funereal spectacle of these youngsters? They return home stupefied on Sunday dawn, drop like zombies onto the bed, cannot see the sun in the day of the Lord or share the joy of being together with their families? The day of light has become for them the day of darkness; the day of life has changed to the day of death; the day of the Lord has been transformed into the day of evil.

It seems appropriate to point out in a more detailed manner another deception in which Satan takes possession of our children using their free time. I want to refer to free sex. On this subject there is in sermons and in the ordinary catechesis of many men of the Church a silence which astonishes. It is treated as if lust were not one of the seven capital vices. There is no doubt that through sexual disorders Satan brings to ruin a great part of our youth, impeding them from discovering the beauty of God's design on love and sexuality and thereby on matrimony and the family.

The Madonna in Medjugorje hasn't failed to give the six visionaries and through them all young people, precise reminders to help them not be seduced by a society immersed in the most miserable immorality in the history of the world. During human history there have always existed sexual disorders, even the most serious, but never has it come to the exaltation of free sex as it has in these times. Immorality is praised and virtue is mocked by the garish power of the mass media. In the past evil was hidden, today it is exhibited. When shame disappears, disrespect rages everywhere. Vileness and obscenity are the hailed masters of our youth.

The image with which the Madonna has characterized hell frightened me very much. In addition to the persons which enter the fire and are transformed into horrible animals, the image which has struck the visionaries the most is the figure of a young woman with long blond hair, undoubtedly the symbol of those who commits sins of lust. The visionary Marija says: "Finally we saw hell. We saw something like a great fire at the centre of which was a young and very beautiful girl who entered this fire and then came out, becoming similar to a beast…"

Vicka who with Jakov was brought physically by the Madonna to see paradise, purgatory and hell, uses much more colourful language, but identical in substance: "In hell…fire…devils…the most ugly people! Everyone with horns and a tail. They all seem to be demons. They suffer. God preserve us from it, enough. I did not recognize anyone. Only I saw that evil blond woman again with horns. She suffers in the middle of that fire; and the devils around her. Horrible and enough!" The first time Vicka had seen this "evil woman" had been when some time before, the Madonna had shown hell in a vision to her, Marija and Jakov.

Mirjana in turn has been a central character of a very singular experience which I have not heard from her lips but from Vicka who has retold it many times to the pilgrims. While she was preparing for the apparition of the Madonna, suddenly a young man with attractive features appeared to her. He was trying to persuade Mirjana not to follow the Madonna and her messages and, on the contrary, was urging her to enjoy her worldly life. Mirjana was having a difficult time looking at him but then she reacted and repelled him very decisively. Shortly after the Madonna appeared to her and explained to her how Satan tries to attract us by presenting himself under seductive appearances.

Mirjana during an apparition.

On first sight it seems to be a story of other periods, scarcely credible to present-day humanity. In reality, by means of this episode, the Madonna demonstrates that she knows the dangers which our young people face very well. With much skill they are dragged on the road of evil by bad companions. They allow themselves to be easily persuaded by their peers to follow the easy and wide road along which they search in vain for liberty and happiness.

How do we react as we face this daunting work of seduction which is unfurled by the contemporary world? How do we react to the force and the shrewdness in which the enemy functions? What weapons do we use to win the battle and bring youth back to God?

PRAYER, EXAMPLE, LOVE

The Madonna doesn't limit herself to making us aware of the difficult situation of the young in the contemporary world and placing them on guard of the perils they meet. In her messages, she even suggests the means to prevent their wandering and to help them find the road again when they are lost.

The focal point is the family. Parents are responsible for the formation of the children before all. They are the ones who, beginning when the children are very small, need to educate them in the faith and in prayer: *"Dear children! — urges the Madonna — Today I call you to renew prayer in your families. Dear children, encourage the very young*

163

to prayer and the children to go to Holy Mass." (March 7/85) The family is that domestic church where youngsters learn to open themselves to God and to live in a Christian way. This work of the family cannot be substituted, even though later on the road of faith finds its natural outlet in the parish.

On this point there should be much to reflect. In fact, in families we should all pray together, parents and children. Every day we should read some verses of the Bible. In this way our children would have their daily spiritual nourishment, without which faith weakens and dies. In reality, in many of our families, even in Christian ones, we are preoccupied with many things like health, studies, clothes and the entertainment of our youngsters. But education in prayer, formation in virtue and the Christian life, is lacking. Our youngsters grow well-fed but spiritually malnourished.

The Madonna reminds parents of three fundamental duties regarding their children: teaching, example and dialogue. Teaching above all concerns prayer. Parents need to teach their children how to pray and need to pray with them. We know how much the Madonna has insisted on this point, even to threatening not to give any more messages if her invitation to pray in the family is not accepted.

In addition, parents need to teach the faith, drawing from the same spring of faith which is the word of God: *"Little children, place the Sacred Scripture in a visible place in your family, and read and live it. Teach your children, because if you are not an example to them, children depart into godlessness."* (Aug. 25/96)

Here the Queen of Peace touches a very painful point. It isn't possible to educate children in the faith if the parents are not themselves committed to a road of faith. How can we pretend that children are ardent Christians when the parents are apathetic Christians? How can the children pray if the parents don't pray? How can children open themselves to God if parents have banished Him from their lives? How can children appreciate the spiritual life if parents are only preoccupied with the material life?

In the first place it is the parents who need to nourish their faith by reading the Bible and living it. After which they will be in a position to communicate to their children something alive, which will inevitably interest them and attract them. The Madonna makes an affirmation which by itself is worth a discourse of pedagogy: *"If you are not an example for them, in the absence of God, children will fall away."* And

164

Marija Pavlovic-Lunetti with her family.

here she gives us a picture of the crisis of faith in our time with impressive precision. This generation has betrayed the great values of the faith, having let themselves be pulled away by consumerism, our youth has strayed far from home, without God.

Prayer, teaching, example and finally dialogue…the Madonna has emphasized this idea in several messages given to Ivan's group. He is the visionary who perhaps most insists on focusing on the problems of youth and the family as he reveals the messages to pilgrims. I remember a message given after a prayer meeting on the mountain. There the Madonna was inviting parents and children to talk together in the family. In the message the Queen of Peace especially requested that parents listen to the life experiences of their children so they could counsel and comfort them.

Even in this case the Madonna in her sublime wisdom of mother, touches a painful point in the life of our families where there is little dialogue and even estrangement between parents and children. In this way our homes become hotels where each one lives his own life, not caring about the others.

It is clear that the first dialogue has to happen between the parents themselves who must build their life as a couple day after day. If the parents are in harmony, their dialogue with their children is easier and much more fruitful. When in the evening the family is at the table together, it is beautiful to exchange reciprocally the experiences of the day, advising and helping each other and then ending with prayer and thanking God. In this way, the family becomes a community where there is joy, peace and faith.

However the reality in the majority of families is quite different. The spiritual life is extinguished, dialogue is dead and the children are distant. What to do? It is necessary that he who has received the grace of conversion begin with great humility, silence and perseverance in his spiritual road. The conversion of a person is a great grace for the whole family. Touched by God, sometimes it can be a son who brings the parents to the road of faith.

Today many families need to be rebuilt and many young people brought again onto the straight road. The Madonna confirms that it is possible only *"with prayer and with love."* The parents who suffer for the children, who have fallen away from God, are not unarmed. They must not forget that God is the Lord of hearts and that His grace can reawaken persons to life who were spiritually dead. If Satan is strong, the Madonna is infinitely stronger, and with the help of our prayers she can bring our children back onto the road of salvation: *"Satan is very strong — she says — therefore, I ask you to dedicate your prayers to me so that those who are under his influence can be saved."* (Feb. 25/88) *"You know, dear children, that with your help I am able to accomplish everything and force Satan not to be seducing [you] to evil and to remove himself from this place."* (Sept. 4/86)

When our youngsters have fallen away on the way of sin, let us keep them constantly under the protection of prayer. Grace already works silently in their lives without their being aware of it. Besides prayer, 'love' is necessary. We need to have the gaze of divine compassion on many poor young people who have been seduced by the diabolical deception and are prisoners of sin. They are people who are spiritually ill and who need to be cured with all the resources of Christian charity.

Sometimes from necessity, love needs to be strong and challenging. The important thing is that it is love. In Medjugorje everyone knows the "Field of Life" where about a hundred young people live. There are different nationalities of youngsters under the firm and wise guidance of Sister Elvira. They were lives destroyed by drugs and without any hope of salvation. A firm hand placed them on their knees, even if they had no faith. An iron rule of life has given them back the lost vigour of youth. The love of a community has made hope flower again.

Even our lost children can find themselves embracing the faith again. Prayer, love and grace can accomplish this miracle. The civilization of love will be born from the new families formed by the youth consecrated to Mary.

CHAPTER 17

Become my joyfully extended hands

THE MADONNA ASKS FOR HELP

Why do fervent Christians, also those who are tepid and even those who are distant, crowd the shrines of the world? The most common motivation is the request for graces, both spiritual and temporal. The prayer of petition is born spontaneously from the heart of people in need of everything. It is right that this be so. In fact which child in moments of necessity does not turn to his father and mother from whom he is sure of receiving help? We also can't say that gratitude and prayers of thanksgiving are lacking when we stop to look at the innumerable objects adorning the walls of many shrines left as offerings in fulfillment of a vow.

Medjugorje makes no exception to this prayer of petition. Perhaps, more than anywhere else, more than anything, the grace of conversion and eternal salvation of the soul, either for themselves or their dear ones, is invoked. Nevertheless, there is something greater and different which marks it. Here it's not only the faithful who appeal for the help of the Madonna but it is she who sadly asks us to help her. The Queen of Peace has come to give but also to ask. From her heart comes the most insistent and dramatic request for help which heaven has addressed to the earth in our time.

A few decades ago a film was made, now almost ignored, whose title "God Needs Men" awakened a great public interest. The idea regarded the necessity of the priest as intermediary between God and man. In reality this assertion has a much more vast theological significance. In fact God needs mankind to complete the entire work of Redemption. To spread the gospel of salvation to the farthest borders of the earth, Jesus Christ did not choose angels but men. God saves man with his co-operation. Mankind needs heaven but heaven also calls all of mankind.

Mary is the unsurpassed co-operator of God. The eternal handmaid has always done and does what her Lord asks. Her arrival in Medjugorje is in obedience to the command of the Omnipotent who sent her. Nevertheless, already from the first messages, the Madonna makes us understand that her presence is not only that of the mother who wants to help and console her children but also and, above all, the guide who comes to gather her army for the great battle so that *"good overcome evil."* (July 25/95)

It needs to be said that the pilgrims swiftly notice this special climate of Medjugorje as if they could breathe it in the air. When we return from any shrine, even in cases where spiritual fruits have been abundant, it rarely happens what is possible to notice in the pilgrims who return from Medjugorje. They feel the insuppressible need to testify and to engage other people in their experience.

Just like the Samaritan woman who, already at the beginning of her road to conversion became a missionary among her fellow citizens, so those devoted to the Gospa become spontaneously and joyously her witnesses all over the world. Thinking about it well, even this book is born of the intimate necessity to communicate something great to those who do not know about it. If it is true that whoever goes to Medjugorje feels called, it can equally be said that he feels sent. The dissemination of the message of the Queen of Peace in the world could not be explained without this particular experience which transforms pilgrims into missionaries.

The Madonna announces her plan from the beginning. She had affirmed in the first Thursday message that she had chosen the parish of Medjugorje especially, to guide it, to protect it and to make it hers. (March 1/84) In the second, she explains the ultimate goals of this selection: *"Dear children, you in the parish, be converted...that all those who shall come here shall be able to convert."* (March 8/84) The parishioners are invited on the road of conversion so they can, in their turn, become instruments of salvation for those far from God.

The boldness of this plan has always struck me, taking into consideration the smallness and the near insignificance of the means. What could a small Croatian village do, which was, among other things, made up of poor farmers isolated from the world and imprisoned in the steel cage of communism? What strategy could have begun from such an insignificant place and with such a simple, ordinary army? I was thinking that it happened like this even the first time. The place where it began was Nazareth, an obscure village on the periphery of the Roman Empire and the conquering army was made up of a carpenter and a few fishermen.

168

Vicka Ivankovic-Mijatovic with husband at baptism of their child.

How many times, I reflected to myself in those first years of the great challenge coming from heaven, had the same event repeated itself in the course of history! Had it not perhaps also happened with St.Benedict, St. Francis, St. Ignatius and St. John Bosco? Places like Guadalupe, Lourdes, Fatima — were they not also forgotten locations in world geography? How many small mustard seeds had become luxuriant trees in the garden of God? "Will it be this way with Medjugorje?" I asked myself in the first years when I was going to Medjugorje bumping over those roads full of holes and surrounded by fields cultivated with tobacco.

Crossing the fields, I would come across poor Croatian women bent by labour and burned by the sun while they were dragging the little cows to pasture and my mind would go spontaneously to the message of the Queen of Peace: *"Dear children, without you I am not able to help the world. I desire that you cooperate with me in everything, even in the smallest things."* (Aug. 28/86) If the Madonna wants to influence the world, why does she not appear to the President of the United States or to some international political assembly where the great who decide the fate of humanity come together?

Is it possible, I said to myself, that to let her Immaculate Heart triumph in this world submerged in evil, (Sept. 25/91) the Madonna needs to knock on the door of a fist full of houses growing among rocks and thorny shrubs where the inhabitants live with sheep, goats and chickens? But my thoughts went to Bethlehem, to that cave where the

Son of God was born and to those simple shepherds, witnesses of the first announcement of heavenly peace.

Who among the pilgrims does not remember Vicka's 90+ year-old grandmother? She was always sitting there in the kitchen, being watched over because when you least expected it, she would run away no one knew where, not even herself. The family would take turns to help her in the middle of that infinite coming and going. People would enter and she would greet them all without knowing anyone, never ceasing to pray. Was she also part of Gospa's army? For our society the aged are a burden. In Mary's line-up they are placed in the first line: *"Dear children, you are forgetting that you are all important. The elderly are especially important in the family. Urge them to pray."* (April 24/86)

Then to escape the impression that her troops are formed of adults, the Madonna in the same message turns to the young: *"Let all the young people be an example to others by their life and let them witness to Jesus."* (April 24/86) In short, none of the inhabitants of the village are excluded. No one can excuse himself.

In Mary's plans, this handful of farming families is the nerve of an army whose goal is to reconquer the world which has abandoned God: *"Dear children, I want you to comprehend that God has chosen each one of you, in order to use you in His great plan for the salvation of mankind. You are not able to comprehend how great your role is in God's design."* (Jan. 25/87)

Have they understood? In all the years that I've been to Medjugorje, I've seen the people live ordinary lives. The population has not lost its head, nor has it yielded to any form of religious fanaticism. It has tried to improve its conditions of life. There are those who have sold fields, those who have built their house with additional rooms for the pilgrims, those who have also set up small stores. I have asked myself many times, how many have engaged themselves with God's plans for the parish and its people? (Nov. 25/87)

And yet, almost without their knowledge, without doing anything extraordinary, Medjugorje has become one of those spiritual centres in the world and one of the most active and bountiful fountains of the new evangelization. What those farming families have done is they have accepted the Queen of Peace in their lives, letting her guide them. This is enough for the Queen of Peace so everyone who goes to Medjugorje can meet her and accept her in their turn. With this spiritual influence, thanks to which Mary enters into anyone's life, she carries forward her plan to *"renew the world."* (Oct. 25/96)

WE ARE ALL IMPORTANT

There is no doubt that even in its smallness in size and elements of human weakness, Medjugorje is a chosen vessel. The same choice of the six youngsters belongs within the divine plan of the parish. The whole community has been called to co-operate with a design of salvation of universal significance. In this sense Medjugorje is something unique and unprecedented. To my knowledge there doesn't exist a similar case in preceding apparitions of the Madonna. Even if the Mother of God only appears to the six youngsters, in reality the entire parish is called to co-operate with a project which concerns the Church and humanity.

All the inhabitants are invited and all are involved. Each one will have to answer personally to the Madonna and to her Son Jesus on the way he has lived and testified the messages. (Feb. 6/86) The Queen of Peace is very explicit about this: *"Little children, I invite each one of you to help my plan to be realized through this parish."* (April 25/94) The parish she has chosen is, in fact, *"... special and different from others."* (Feb. 6/86)

Now that Medjugorje has become a world centre of spirituality and prayer, Mary continues to manifest a particular care for the parish. She liked to clarify that she gives the messages first to the parishioners and then to everyone else. (Feb. 6/86) *"God wants this parish —* she says, making an appeal to the will of the Omnipotent *— to belong completely to Him. And that's what I want too."* (Feb. 28/85)

I don't know to what point Medjugorje is aware of this singular and very important selection. I have hardly ever heard it spoken of, either by the visionaries, the people or in the sermons. And yet the messages of the Queen of Peace about this are numerous, explicit and even sorrowful. One could get the impression that the people of the place feel an instinctive fear facing an assignment out of proportion of its strength. The Madonna is aware that they do not understand: *"You are not able to comprehend how great your role is in God's design. Therefore, dear children, pray so that in prayer you may be able to comprehend what God's plan is in your regard,"* (Jan. 25/87) but then she encourages them with words of consolation: *"I am with you so that you can bring everything to reality."* (Jan. 25/87)

In substance, what does the Madonna ask of the inhabitants of that small village of Herzegovina so they can become instruments for the conversion of the world? What do they have to do that is special to realize a project of such vast proportions? They have to put the messages into practice. Mary invites them to begin a way of conversion and of returning to God so that everyone that she calls to Medjugorje could be helped on the road to conversion. *"Dear children! Today I call you all to pray that God's plans for us may be realized and also everything that God desires through you! Help others to be converted, especially those who are coming to Medjugorje."* (Jan. 30/86)

On closer reflection, the parish community is not invited to accomplish who knows what extraordinary enterprises. Reasonably, the Madonna asks more than once that it remain in its littleness and humility (June 28/85) so that Satan does not seduce it with his pride and his false strength. (Nov. 25/87) In the end, what the people have to do is to begin a walk of faith and prayer, of sacrifice and conversion so that in the life of each one, the simplicity and beauty of Christian holiness will shine forth.

In effect, the impression that one has staying in Medjugorje is that of a most ordinary Christian life. The people live the normal practice of the sacraments and the commandments. I haven't seen in the parish evidence of those particular spiritual favours of which many Christians in the world chase. The Madonna wants her parish to be a model of simple Christianity and available to all, where the essential thing is the presence of God in the heart. The way of holiness until love is perfected is accomplished through the often apparently monotonous and insignificant duties and obligations of everyday life.

This is what the Madonna asks for, first of the parishioners and then of all the others: *"Dear*

A local villager at prayer.

172

children, I am giving the messages first of all to the residents of the parish, and then to all the others." (Feb. 6/86) This is Mary's plan in all her grandiose simplicity. She asks a small parish in the world to begin the walk of conversion so that everyone who comes on pilgrimage in turn is converted.

Probably better parishes than Medjugorje exist in Christianity. It would be a misrepresentation to believe that Mary's community is flawless and without defects. I myself have met many young people further ahead on the road to sanctity than the six visionaries who still see the Madonna every day. However, what makes Medjugorje unique is the grace of selection. God doesn't necessarily choose the best or the most saintly. But those who have been chosen receive a special grace to carry out the task.

What is the special grace given to Medjugorje? It is that of being the parish in which the Mother of God is present. By accepting her in their lives and trying hard to live out her messages, the parishioners help everyone who comes there to meet Mary and to begin their walk of conversion.

We can find Christian communities which enlighten us with their zeal even in other places. But to my knowledge, there doesn't exist any place on earth where the special grace of conversion is granted in such a special way. Medjugorje is a community which heaven calls to convert itself in order to become an instrument of conversion and salvation for the entire world: *"I invite you to open yourselves completely to me so that, through each one of you, I can convert and save this world which is full of sin and bad things."* (Aug. 25/92)

But if the responsibility of the parishioners is great before God, (Feb. 6/86) it is no less of those whom the Queen of Peace calls to Medjugorje. To this village, once insignificant and unknown, arrive pilgrims from the whole world. The name of Medjugorje is universally known. This uninterrupted flow of travelers thirsty for peace enters again into a divine project. It is a fact that from 1981, a world parish which Mary protects under her mantle has become her invisible weapon. Its assignment, to realize her project of bringing the world back to God, has formed around Medjugorje.

In a certain sense, all the pilgrims who have heard the call and have responded to the invitation have entered this great Marian community of the Queen of Peace. Through the testimony of her messages, they have become instruments of her maternal presence in the world. All those who have been to Medjugorje and have responded to the grace, accepting Mary as a guide in the walk of sanctity, carry out an irreplaceable task in God's plan. Even they, like the parishioners, will have to answer to the Madonna and to her Son.

In a particular way the messages of the last years, always bearing in mind that Medjugorje is an irreplaceable oasis of peace, rang over Mary's global parish, which now has become an unstoppable river of love: *"Dear children! Today I invite you to become missionaries of my messages, which I am giving here through this place that is dear to me. God has allowed me to stay this long with you and therefore, little children, I invite you to live with love the messages I give and to transmit them to the whole world, so that a river of love flows to people who are full of hatred and without peace. I invite you, little children, to become peace where there is no peace and light where there is darkness, so that each heart accepts the light and the way of salvation."* (Feb. 25/95)

A river always has a source. It is the maternal heart of Mary, present and alive in Medjugorje. From there the waters of peace and joy spread over all the earth, through the hearts which have met her, welcomed her and loved her. Her appeal cannot but shake us: *"I invite you, little children, to help me through your prayers so that as many hearts as possible come close to my Immaculate Heart."* (May 25/95) *"In the end my Immaculate Heart will triumph,"* the Madonna at Fatima had prophesied. That prophesy today is realized even through each of us, co-operating with the Queen of Peace in the work of the salvation of the world.

IN HELPING OTHERS YOU WILL FIND SALVATION

The Kingdom of God is like a mustard seed, Jesus says. "It is the smallest of the seeds but once grown, it is larger than the other legumes and becomes a tree so that the birds of the air come and make their nests in its branches." (Matt 13, 31) Here we see the story of a village which becomes an enclosed world cenacle, where Mary gathers the new apostles of the faith, love and peace under her mantle. On the occasion of the anniversary of the apparitions, and considering the great response, with true maternal kindness, the Madonna thanked everyone especially for answering the call: *"Today I desire to thank you* — she said — *for living my messages."* (June 25/98)

Today, the Queen of Peace organizes an army of faithful through which she can let *"the God of peace and joy"* be known *"to the whole world."* (March 25/88) The expressions with which the Madonna addresses those at her service are extraordinarily, beautiful and effective. In a certain sense we almost have the impression of participating in the unique and unrepeatable experience of the first apostles. How can we not feel chosen, appreciated, valued and loved when the Madonna invites us to be the *"missionaries of the messages," "the joyous bringers of peace,"* the *"apostles of faith," "the outstretched hands of God,"* the *"witnesses of joy," "the salt of the earth, the light of the world,"* and the *"sign of the love of God?"*

In a growing measure, the messages of the last years show the universal outlines of Mary's plan. *"Through you* — she affirms turning to those devoted to her — *I wish to renew the world."* (Oct. 25/96) How is this possible? What must those who have answered the call and want to be the instruments for the conversion and salvation of the world do?

We do not need to imagine great things like St. Paul already cautioned. The Queen of Peace asks us only one thing: *"open yourselves completely to me."* (Aug. 25/92) Let her be the guide and the teacher of her spiritual journey in such a way that we are hers without reservation. When Mary is alive in us, wherever we are and wherever we go, let us diffuse the perfume of her presence and be instruments of her love toward all men.

One of the most beautiful messages about this was given to us on the day of the Annunciation when the beautiful news of salvation rang out for the first time: *"Dear children! Today I rejoice with you and I invite you to open yourselves to me, and become an instrument in my hands for the salvation of the world. I desire, little children, that all of you who have felt the odor of holiness through these messages which I am giving you to carry, to carry it into this world, hungry for God and God's love. I thank you all for having responded in such a number and I bless you all with my motherly blessing."* (March 25/94)

The Madonna more than once underlines that the apostolic method which she wants us to use to bring back those fallen away from God is that of examples and works. We bring peace if we are in peace. We bring love if we live in love. We bring God if we have God in our hearts. *"I do not desire* — she cautions — *your life to pass by in words but that you glorify God with deeds."* (April 25/91)

In other words, Mary proposes that method of apostolate that was hers during her earthly life. Through the ordeals of daily life, she brought the divine presence everywhere. Mary's apostolic style is accessible to all and her silent dispersal is an irresistible force: *"I therefore call and ask* — she encourages us — *that by your lives and by your daily living you witness my presence."* (June 25/91)

Each of us must firstly let Mary be present in our hearts and let her shape it into the image of her Immaculate Heart. If Mary is in us, wherever we are, even in the most hostile places or among people who are the most distant, we become the sign of her presence. In our smallness and through grace we become instruments which transmit her smile, her light, her peace and her joy. In this very simple way, founded on the example of life, we become hands joyously extended by which the Queen of Peace brings God to a world which has lost Him.

In this time, which through Mary *"is united to heaven in a special way,"* we are called to change from half-heartedness to *"being active,"* *"collaborating with life and with our example in the work of salvation."* (May 25/96)

"Children — the Queen of Peace repeats without fatigue — *I wish that all people convert and see me and my son, Jesus, in you...In helping the other, your soul will also find salvation."* (May 25/96)

For having collaborated in this great plan there will be no lack of rewards, the greatest possible and imaginable. *"Sacrifice your lives for the salvation of the world ... but* — the Madonna promises — *in heaven you shall receive the Father's reward which He has promised to you."* (Feb. 25/88)

CHAPTER 18

I desire to save all souls and bring them to God

I WISH THAT THE LORD WOULD ALLOW ME TO CLARIFY THE SECRETS, AT LEAST IN PART

It would be superficial and dangerous to undervalue the theme of the secrets which make up a part of the messages of Medjugorje. About their existence and importance, there is the agreed testimony of the six visionaries. Mirjana, Ivanka and Jakov who know all ten affirm that in the apparition which they have regularly once a year, the Madonna has reflected on this topic on different occasions. From 1987, the Queen of Peace has said through Mirjana that it would be her wish for the Lord to permit her to illuminate us on the secrets. Yet it is a question of a grace which we are quite far from meriting. (message to Mirjana, May 28/87) [5]

Nevertheless, many approach this theme in apocalyptic terms, pressed on by a morbid curiosity. Today there is no lack of messages which suggest the end of the world or that describe the future in catastrophic colours. This atmosphere is absolutely far from the spirit and the reality of Medjugorje. The Madonna has never spoken about the end of the world and her coming is to instruct and guide us, and not to frighten us, as the visionaries all affirm in agreement.

The fact that the Mother of God has confided some secrets to chosen persons who will speak to the world, need not surprise us. It has already happened in other apparitions approved by the Church. The most noted case is that of Fatima. Even Jesus, in a certain sense, proceeded in the same way when for example, coming down from Mt. Tabor, he ordered Peter, James and John not to tell anyone what they had seen until after the Son of man had risen from the dead. (Mark 9, 9)

The secrets tied to the apparitions of Medjugorje are ten. Only Mirjana, Ivanka and Jakov know them all, while Vicka, Marija and Ivan know nine. The secrets concern the future. Some deal with the personal lives of the youngsters, others Medjugorje, others the whole world. It is thought that the more important ones are the same for all while the personal ones are different.

Of all the secrets, something regarding the third is known. The visionaries speak about a sign the Madonna will leave on Podbrdo, on the place of the first apparitions. It will be a visible sign, indestructible, long lasting and beautiful. Its purpose will be to confirm the apparitions of the Mother of God in Medjugorje and, at the same time, it will create an extreme appeal to conversion. Mirjana also affirms that, thanks to the prayers and fasting of those who have answered the call, the punishment of God forecasted by the seventh secret has been appeased.

Mirjana in particular, regarding the secrets concerning the near future of the world, confirms that she knows exactly what it is about and when it will happen. She has chosen a priest, the Franciscan priest Father Petar Ljubicic, to whom to confide them ten days before they will be verified so that he can make them public to everyone.

Once established that the theme of the secrets is serious and once clarified that they are not about the end of the world, there are immediate questions. How to try to answer them in a convincing way: will these events concerning the future of humanity necessarily happen or only under determined conditions?

When Vicka was questioned by Father Bubalo if every secret would be realized, she answered: "Not necessarily. For this the Madonna has said that we need to pray and fast to moderate the anger of God."

The subjective characteristics of some of the secrets are demonstrated by the statement of the Queen of Peace regarding the seventh secret which was appeased because of prayer and fasting. In other words, whether certain events will happen or not depends on us and on our response to the appeal of conversion.

The Madonna lets us understand this even from some of her messages. For example, she states: *"God sends me to you out of love, that I may help you to comprehend that without Him there is no future or joy and, above all, there is no eternal salvation."* (April 4/97) Choosing the way of evil, it is humanity which inflicts the greatest punishments on itself, compromising its future in time and in eternity. On the other hand, even concerning the war, which began to flare up in the ex Yugoslavia, the Madonna said: *"much of what will happen depends on your prayers and you are praying a little bit."* (July 25/91)

What does all of this mean? It means that the future depends on us, on our response to the call. If there is a strong embrace of her appeal to conversion, if humanity will return to God, then it will enter into a new time of peace without facing a new major tribulation. Otherwise, because we have not wanted to listen to the language of love, God will necessarily use the language of sorrow to save our souls.

We are not facing a message of threats but a maternal reminder of profound evangelical inspiration. Even Jesus had placed His contemporaries on guard, saying to them: *"If you do not repent, you will all perish."* (Luke 13,3) It wasn't God who sent the Roman legions which destroyed Jerusalem, but it was the fanatics of the earthly messiah who brought upon themselves the tremendous calamity. In the same way, without returning to God, the modern world creates the basis, already visible today, for its self-destruction.

Therefore it could also happen that some secrets remain such, because the Madonna has obtained the response which was expected. We hope that it will be like this; in fact we must behave so that it will not be necessary to reveal them. But when they will be known, then *"it will be too late."* (to Mirjana, Jan. 28/87)

I am compelled to underline the profound connection that exists between the theme of the secrets and the principal message which the Madonna has given in Medjugorje, that of conversion. (Feb. 25/96) The primary objective of the Virgin is that of bringing back to God a world which deceives itself to be able to do without Him. The Madonna cautions us that without God there is no future and the road to ruin is open before a humanity which believes it can find fulfillment without its Creator. In the secrets regarding the future of the world, the Queen of Peace shows what will happen if man persists on the *"bad road"* of evil and sin.

It is a matter of how we see prophetic reminders which have precedents in Sacred Scripture. By order of the Lord, Jonah made this proclamation to the city of Nineveh whose malice had risen to the skies: "Another forty days and Nineveh will be destroyed." (Jonah 3,3) It would seem to be an absolute declaration without any possibility of escape. Perhaps the prophet intended it to be so. But the population understood that it was an appeal to conversion and was penitent, thinking: "Who knows if God will not change his mind and relent, if He will not renounce His burning wrath so that we do not perish?" Effectively things went exactly like that. In fact Scripture affirms: "God saw their efforts to renounce their evil behavior. And God relented: he did not inflict on them the disaster which he had threatened." (Jonah 3,10)

The real problem is to know if our generation is disposed to behave like the inhabitants of Nineveh. However, it depends on us, on our good will. The sensation nevertheless is that our times are more susceptible to the enticements of seduction than to the invitations of conversion.

GOD'S PROJECTS ARE PEACE PROJECTS

In closing this book a question must be asked: what is in store for us in the future? Is it possible to understand what awaits us in the third millennium from the messages of Medjugorje? In spite of the seriousness of the reprimands implied in some secrets, we can affirm that the divine project which the Madonna is bringing to fruition is full of mercy and love for this poor world.

We don't know if God will be compelled to use the language of sorrow to bring us back to the road of salvation in the near future or in what measure He will have to do it. It is certain however that the final outcome of the divine plan will be "the new world of peace." Let's not forget that the Madonna has come as the Queen of Peace. She has come to be victorious and to prepare with us *a new time, a time which God gives you as grace so that you may get to know him more.*" (Jan. 25/98)

The key message about this is when the Mother of God names another apparition for the first and only time, that of Fatima. Here she

says openly that she wants to complete what was begun at Fatima with our help: *"I invite you — she says — to self-renunciation for nine days so that, with your help, everything that I desire to realize through the secrets I began in Fatima, may be fulfilled."* (Aug. 8/91)

At the beginning of the 20th century of the "great tribulation" as John Paul II defined it, Mary appeared at Fatima to confirm her maternal presence in a world which was sinking into darkness and in the shadow of death. Her prophecy intersects this endless night of evil like a sheaf of light until it indicates the certain triumph of her Immaculate Heart.

At the end of the century, through Medjugorje, Mary brings to completion what she had started in Fatima. She does so with a great new appeal for conversion and in this way prepares a future of peace and joy in which we will live reconciled to God and among ourselves: *"I invite you — she begs — to open yourselves completely to me so that, through each one of you, I can convert and save this world."* (Aug. 25/92) *"I call you all to build a new world of peace with me through prayer."* (Dec. 25/92) *"I invite you — she repeats — open yourselves to me, and become an instrument in my hands for the salvation of the world."* (Jan. 25/98)

When will this happen? We don't know but there is no doubt that what the Queen of Peace intends to carry out with our help will be accomplished in the end. Much will depend on our collaboration, but it is certain that heaven is in a hurry to flood the earth with love and mercy: *"Pray so that a time of peace which my heart waits for impatiently, will reign as soon as possible."* (April 24/97)

This 'impatience' of the Madonna so that the triumph of her Immaculate Heart will happen as soon as possible strikes us. Of what does this final appeal consist, this triumph prophesied at Fatima and which is discussed so much? It is a matter of the return of humanity to God. Will this happen? Yes, this will happen of course; we hope soon, without the need of God letting man taste further how bitter and unbearable life is away from Him.

I would like to underline the perfect harmony of the project of the Queen of Peace with the pastoral actions of John Paul II taken in view of the Great Jubilee of the Year 2000. The Pope dissolved any millennial fear and indicated the way toward the time of joy for the feast of the birthday of Jesus Christ (Jubilee means Joy). It is a question of the way of conversion, of repentance and purification. In this way the door which introduces us to the third millennium will be crossed with the excitement of one who sees in the horizon the new civilization of love which God will give as grace to a converted humanity.

Medjugorje indicates a great potential of light which shines on a new world of peace; not a human peace, but a divine peace, which already foresees the joy of paradise here on earth in the hearts of men. Will our generation see this world? We do not know and this is not the most important thing.

Now we find ourselves in a difficult situation immersed *"world which is full of sin and bad things."* (Aug. 25/92) In the message recalling Fatima, the Madonna invites us *"to understand the importance of her coming and the seriousness of the situation."* Our task now is to respond to the call and to do the work of the heart to separate us from a life of sin and place ourselves on the road to sanctity. In this way we will prepare a new world for ourselves and for our children.

Nevertheless, the ultimate destination to look for is not mankind's future in time but its end in eternity. The civilization of love is the reflection of heaven on earth. Our ultimate goal however, is heaven. There, the Mother of God wants to bring all her children. No one is excluded: *"I desire* — she affirms with the impetus of love — *I want to save all souls and present them to God."* (Aug. 25/91) And also: *"Little children* — she says with tenderness — *I am your mother, I love you and I desire that each of you be saved and thus be with me in Heaven."* (Aug. 25/98)

Will this great message of salvation be fulfilled? Yes, but by means of our personal conversion and our active and persevering co-operation. This time of great grace will not be repeated again if this is how the pronouncement of the Madonna is to be understood as reported by all six visionaries: *"These are my last apparitions on earth."* Now Mary is with us as she has never been in the past and as she will never again be in the future. We must answer today if we don't want to be sad tomorrow otherwise the Lord who passes has knocked on the door of our hearts in vain.

One of the greatest graces granted to Christianity in our generation is to have Mary beside us for such a long time on our journey of life and human history: *"I am with you and I guide you into a new time, a time which God gives you as grace so that you may get to know him more."* (Jan. 25/93) Do we not want to take advantage of, and seize this unique and unprecedented occasion?

MEDJUGORJE IN THE CHURCH, WITH THE CHURCH AND FOR THE CHURCH

The apparitions of the Madonna in Medjugorje are a great gift from God to humanity, but in a particular way to the Church. On May 13, 1981 Pope John Paul II was nearly shot to death. Satan in his blindness did not notice the fact of the date of the first apparition of the Virgin at Fatima. Or perhaps he chose it on purpose, as a gesture of daring. The Madonna saved the Pope and used the plan of evil to carry out her projects prepared so long ago. John Paul II quickly understood the meaning of the event and brought to Fatima the bullet which should have killed him. From that day, he became even more Mary's Pope since she had saved his life for the Church.

A little more than a month later, on June 24th of the same year, on the feast of St. John the Baptist, forerunner of Christ and prophet of conversion, the Madonna began her apparitions in Medjugorje. Even she, like the Baptist, invites us to conversion and prepares our hearts to receive Christ. In all that time until his passing, the Queen of Peace walked beside John Paul II, speaking a Slavic language like him, anticipating or accompanying his teachings and making him the privileged instrument of the triumph of her Immaculate Heart.

This should be enough to help us grasp the profound connection between the apparitions of Medjugorje and the Church. But more than this, it must be underlined that they are in close connection with a fundamental structure of the Church, which is the parish. It is sustained by the pastoral efforts of a religious order, the Franciscans, in its male and female branches, among the most reputable of Christianity.

Added to this is the influx of pilgrims from every part of the world, in particular that of tens of thousands of priests. The reawakening of faith, the miracle of innumerable conversions, the return to the enthusiasm of the Christian life, the blossoming again of personal and group prayer, the rediscovery of the great value of the sacraments, in particular of the Holy Mass and confession, the spiritual healing of many youth and the sprouting of many vocations to the consecrated life, are fruits that are before the eyes of the whole ecclesial community.

The competent authority of the Church handled the apparitions of Medjugorje in the most prudent and wise way. In this discussion anyone can express personal opinions. The faithful, however, are bound to the official pronouncements of the Church. They leave the faithful free to believe or not to believe and to go to Medjugorje in pilgrimages organized privately. The Church, moreover, with its administrative bodies, continues to follow the events. It surveys it so that the clergy of the area is always conforming to the true Marian spirit.

The Church cannot do any more. Asking for approval before the end of the apparitions would mean going against the most fundamental rules of prudence. Let us let the competent ecclesial authorities do their work, without force and without feeding useless controversies. The Madonna is not at all concerned with this type of problem. She is interested in our spiritual journey. Of what use would an ecclesiastic approval be without conversion? But if there is response to the call, approval will also come in due time.

The testimony that I want to leave the reader at the end of this book is that of an immense gratitude and of a boundless joy for having met Mary in Medjugorje. The Queen of Peace has led me slowly to understand the divine beauty of faith and the inestimable greatness of the gift of life. With her, everything becomes full of light and one remains enraptured in contemplating the infinite love of God in the work of creation and of salvation.

Yes, life with God is marvelous and even in the weariness and in the spiritual combat we can already taste the divine joy here on earth as we wait for the glory, light and happiness of paradise.

THE END...THE BEGINNING

Footnotes

1. The original six visionaries are Vicka Ivankovic (born 1964), Marija Pavlovic-Lunetti (born 1965), Mirjana Dragicevic-Soldo (born 1965), Ivanka Ivankovic (born 1966), Jacov Colo (born 1971), Ivan Dragicevic (born 1965).

2. Mirjana Soldo reported receiving monthly messages on the second of each month in early 2005.

3. "Marija Pavlovic racconta Medjugorje." Ed. Shalon, page 35.

4. "Vicka parla ai giovani e alle famiglie," Ed. Shalom, pages 279-286.

5. J. Bubalo, "Mille incontri con la Madonna," Ed. Messagero, Padova, pages 166-168.

Radio Maria

Radio Maria was founded as a parish radio station 1983, in Arcellasco d'Erba, in the in the Diocese of Milan, Italy.

It was a time when many priests were placing antennas on their bell towers to reach the greatest number of faithful possible, particularly those who were ill. The purpose of the radio was to provide news for parishioners and help them in prayer, by broadcasting the Mass and Rosary.

Radio Maria maintained this characteristic until January 1987, when the Radio Maria association was founded, composed of priests and lay people, with the aim of making the station independent from the parish and involving it in a vaster scale evangelization.

In only three years radio programming was completely redesigned, thanks to the collaboration of individuals with different ecclesiastical backgrounds, but all committed to bearing witness to their faith.

All of the regions of Italy were quickly covered at the same time, so that in 1990 Radio Maria was considered a national radio network.

The radio began expanding to the rest of the world starting in the 1990's. Today there are more than 50 Radio Maria in the world and many others are getting ready to start broadcasting.

The aim is to meet the requests of those from all over the world, in order to create a worldwide Catholic radio network, with independent management for the individual national stations, but united and coherent with a religious inspiration, radio programming organization, reference to volunteering and financing from listener donations.

Radio Maria is a tool of the new evangelization which serves the Church of the Third Millenium, as a Catholic station committed to calling for conversion through radio programming which offers plenty of space for prayer, catechism and human promotion.

It bases its mission on faith in divine providence and depends on volunteer work.

For more information contact: www.RadioMaria.org

Canada: www.hmwn.net. U.S.A.: www.radiomaria.us

Medjugorje Books

Available from the Publisher

Our Lady Speaks from Medjugorje
By Andrew J. Yeung

Revised edition. This book contains the messages of Our Lady of Medjugorje by subject matter from "A" to "Z". Over 100 topics! A handy and quick guide for anyone interested in finding out what Our Lady said about a particular issue.

#1570 160 pp. $7.95

Medjugorje Testament:
Hostility Abounds, Grace Superabounds
By Father René Laurentin

Fr. Laurentin's last in a series of books on the reported apparitions in Medjugorje. The book gives news of the apparitions and visionaries, the position of the authorities, the local bishop, the other bishops, the Pope, the arguments of the opponents, results of scientific tests done on the seers, testimonies, messages and the fruits.

#1545 238 pp. Sale $5.00

Ransomed from Darkness: The New Age, Christian Faith and the Battle for Souls
By Moira Noonan

The author was a New Age church minister for 20 years. Her practice involved clairvoyance, Reiki, hypnotherapy, psychic healing, tarot cards, crystals, reincarnation, channeling, and other occult practices. The Blessed Mother intervened during a visit to Medjugorje, where Moira was 'delivered' Magdalene-style from a series of evil spirits during a 16 hour exorcism. This book chronicles her faith journey back to the Catholic Church and exposes the spiritual dangers of New Age practices so prevalent today.

#1586 238 pp. $16.95

Our Lady Weeps: Report on Civitavecchia
By Bishop Girolamo Grillo

In 1995, a statue brought from Medjugorje reportedly wept tears of blood 14 times in Civitavecchia, Italy (outside Rome). In this book Luciano Lincetto interviews Bishop Grillo, who experienced firsthand an extraordinary event which personally involved him. This book is a kind of official document on the inquiry.

#1565 128 pp. $9.95

A Place of Healing: The Virgin Mary in Medjugorje
By John Dinolfo

This book is a compelling look at 11 of the more than 400 reported healings attributed to Our Lady since 1981. Relying on the facts and medical documents, the author carefully probes the reported healings and how they changed their lives and those around them.

#1510 233 pp. $12.95

Medjugorje: What's Happening?
Fr. James Mulligan

An informative account of the early days of the reported apparitions and subsequent events up to the present controversies, including a synopsis of ten holy places where the Vatican has declared that Marian apparitions took place.

ISBN 978-0-9560609-0-7 **256 pp. color $16.95**

Medjugorje Way of the Cross
Meditations by Fr. Tomislav Ivancic

You will be visually transported to Mount Krizevac as you meditate on each image of the bronze stations. Interspersed are relevant messages from Our Lady of Medjugorje. Colour illustrations.

#145 36pp. $3.95 each; 10 for $24.00; 25 for $50; 100 for $150.